Africa on A Global Stage

Africa on A Global Stage

Editors
Tanya Lyons
and
Geralyn Pye

Africa World Press, Inc.

P.O. Box 1892
Trenton, NJ 08607

P.O. Box 48
Asmara, ERITREA

Africa World Press, Inc.

P.O. Box 1892
Trenton, NJ 08607

P.O. Box 48
Asmara, ERITREA

First printing 2006

Book Design: 'Damola Ifaturoti
Cover Design: Ashraful Haque

Library of Congress Cataloging-in-Publication Data

Africa on a global stage / edited by Tanya Lyons and Geralyn Pye.
p. cm.
Includes bibliographical references and index.
ISBN 1-59221-387-1 (hardcover) -- ISBN 1-59221-388-X (pbk.)
1. Africa--Economic conditions--1960- 2. Africa--Social conditions--1960- 3. Africa--Politics and government--1960- 4. Globalization--Economic aspects--Africa. I. Lyons, Tanya. II. Pye, Geralyn, 1962-

HC800.A558 2005
960.3'3--dc22 2005024846

Table of Contents

Acknowledgements

This book was developed from the themes of the annual African Studies Association of Australasia and the Pacific (AFSAAP) Conference entitled "Africa on A Global Stage: Politics, Economics and Culture", held at Flinders University, Adelaide, South Australia in October 2003. We would like to thank each of the contributors to this volume who prepared their chapters after much debate and discussion in Adelaide. We acknowledge the Faculty of Social Sciences at Flinders University, Adelaide, Australia for a small research Support and Incentive Grant. We would also like to acknowledge Thomas McFarlane for his editorial assistance. Thanks also to all those who make an effort to keep Africa on the political and social map in Australia.

Chapter 1

Africa on A Global Stage: An Introduction

Tanya Lyons and Geralyn Pye

Africa has been discovered, explored, mapped, colonised, decolonised and marginalised, falling off various maps, only to be placed back on maps of horror and human tragedy. Africa has been the dark continent since Conrad's *Heart of Darkness*, with surprisingly few changes to its global stereotype. All this despite recent revolutions in technology (television and the Internet) enabling African images and experiences to filter through to the rest of the world; to educate the 'others' about the diversity and richness of the African continent. Africa is consistently marginalized in time and space through international relations and the global political economy, and it faces challenging prospects on the global stage in relation to globalisation (Lyons 2002). The authors in this volume come from an international and multidisciplinary background, providing a unique and insightful commentary on the current concerns facing Africa in this era of globalisation.

As Kofi Annan (1998: 3-4) has pointed out, the globalisation process involves potential winners and losers:

> On one hand Africa is displaying signs of a transition to emerging market status with all its positive benefits. On the other hand, however, it is still continuing to suffer both from the lingering effects of previous ills (such as debt and SAPs) that produced major economic, social and political problems, and from the new hardships brought on by this newly emerging market status.

Perhaps the argument should be less about winners and losers and more about whether Africans should be asked if and how they want to be involved in globalisation. One might question however, whether and in what ways globalisation permits African participation in its processes (Pieterse 2000).

The formation of the African Union (AU) in July 2000, replacing the cumbersome and overly bureaucratic Organisation of African Unity (OAU), and the signing of the New Partnerships for African Development (NEPAD) in July 2001 might appear to be one way for Africans to participate in globalisation (De Waal 2002). This regional African institution emerged out of the concept of the 'African Renaissance', a term first used in the anti-colonial struggles and recently revived by the President of South Africa, Thabo Mbeki. Mbeki's intentions were to capture those same Pan-African sentiments for progress and development. Yet, he has been criticized by Fantu Cheru (2002: xii) as simply being a part of a South African hegemonic neoliberal project that has no relevance to the rest of Africa. According to Cheru, this 'African Renaissance' is certainly not a plan for the future, offering no framework for change. Yet, it represents one of the 3 responses by African governments to the economic challenges posed by globalisation, identified by Cheru, and which are discussed in the chapters here by Teresa Thorp and Helen Ware.

The first response by some African governments has been

to "embrace globalization uncritically as a development strategy"(Cheru 2002: xv). The second response taken has been to "resist indiscriminate market liberalization and 'coerced' integration into global markets"(Cheru 2002: xv). Both of these responses by African governments demonstrate that globalisation indeed has a stranglehold on Africa with external organisations and international financial institutions heavily influencing local outcomes. Yet, both of these African responses have failed because the state also failed to prevent massive financial crises, and the World Bank and other Western donors responded in turn by imposing conditionalities on loans, and threatening trade and aid sanctions unless African countries complied.

Cheru's central argument is for a different approach to the challenges of globalization, one providing alternatives that would benefit Africa in the global economic exchange. This third response is "*a guided embrace of globalisation with a commitment to resist* through pre-emptive national or regional development strategies and economic policy coordination" (Cheru 2002: xv). Yet, as Helen Ware suggests, in her chapter analyzing poverty reduction programs, perhaps even a guided embrace of globalisation will be unable to reconcile the very effects of the neo-liberal globalisation project on Africa. Some possible consequences of these negative effects are explored both by William Reno (Chapter 9) and ourselves below.

In attempting to locate Africa in the context of globalisation, this book begins with the colonial period and examines the representations of Africa on the global stage that directly influenced the imperial process. We then examine the continuities in representations that challenge notions of dramatic change since the decolonisation of Africa. The impact of social change on individual and national identity is discussed, and sheds some light on the current issues of identity in post-conflict societies in Africa. Whereas ethnicity was central to Rwanda's genocide, Kenya has seen the emergence of non-ethnic cleavages under the influence of global-local contexts. Nothing, however, has had such an impact on the African continent as the theories of modernization and neo-liberalism. We discuss the free trade process and the negative effects of these processes reflected in the failure of Poverty Reduction Programs, and ultimately in the collapse of some African states. Finally, we explore the possible reasons for these failures and suggest some key issues which need to be addressed to give Africa a meaningful role on the global stage.

Jeremy Martens' chapter on *The Impact of Theories of Civilisation and Savagery on Native Policy in Colonial Natal* explores the origins of Africa's location on the global stage. The worldviews shaped by the colonial enterprise placed Africa and Africans somewhere low down on the scale between savagery and civilization, and as we know and acknowledge now, overlooked the complexities of African society especially kinship networks. Nonetheless, as Martens argues here, these forms of colonial rule in Natal are still reflected in current arrangements. The 'rules' are based not only on the pragmatic responses to colonisation described by historians, but also on simplistic British colonial notions of progress, that is, from barbarism to civilization.

Martens' observations of this continuity in the notion of progress are also taken up in Eric Louw's chapter, *Afrikaner and South African Black Nationalism: A Cultural Studies Perspective,* which demonstrates how worldviews are shaped by agenda setters, contributing to a continuity of development progress as shaped by elites. Using a cultural studies perspective, Louw discusses the influence of representations on an individual's worldview. Louw argues that we internalize the representations around us, and embed ourselves into those pictures of the world made available to us. We actively construct our own worldview through a process of engaging with, and drawing upon, linguistic material in our environment, yet ultimately we are influenced by the 'agenda setters' who control the meaning-making institutions, such as the media and schools. Louw points out that it is the ruling elites in the nations in question who are mostly concerned with this 'agenda setting function'. One purpose of such a theoretical exploration of nation and identity building would be to help explain Africa's current socio-political problems and crises. According to Louw, traditional African studies approaches have failed to explain the internal combustion within Africa nations. A cultural studies approach, he argues here, can "provide a method for examining the identities and cultures underpinning Africa's political processes and attempts (successful and failed) at nation building". Louw develops his thesis by applying it to South Africa's experiences of nation building in the twentieth century, shaped by the three models of nation building and modernization: Anglo-settler capitalism; Afrikaner-nationalism; and Black-nationalism. The first, inspired by Lord Milner, led ultimately to apartheid and then Afrikaner-nationalism, which in turn created resistance to apartheid among urbanized and Westernized blacks, and eventually to the mobilization of the African National Congress. Finally, Louw's theories are applied to the rise of the 'Gucci Comrades', South Africa's version of the 'Wabenzi' elite in East Africa (the Swahili term for the 'tribe' that drives Mercedes Benz), and the subsequent increasing gap between them and the black underclass. The former are the beneficiaries of globalisation, the latter its casualties. Louw concludes that the current South African model of development appears eerily similar to the original racist model. He shows clearly through examining dominant discourses of nationalism that there are significant continuities. Thus, to understand Africa on a global stage, and to understand the success or failure of African states under the control of African elites since decolonisation and the end of apartheid in South Africa, a cultural studies perspective can provide us with a methodology for understanding the behaviour of African elites and the continuation of social and economic cleavages that currently demarcate many African societies.

Jane Gilbert, in her chapter *Two Worlds: Integration, Synthesis or Conflict? Psychological Perspectives on Cultural Identity in Africa,* provides a closer examination of the effects of social and cultural change on the individual, arguing that globalisation has increased previously existing threats to individual and national identity. In the African context, individuals need to re-interpret and integrate their past in order to provide a vision for the future. Gilbert considers in particular the conflict of identities in Africa between Western, global and local African influences which can threaten identity and contribute to instability. Political and community leaders need to understand this conflict of identity and be sensitive to the problems an individual may face, in order that leaders can effect the processes of change in ways which are both respectful and humane, and are perhaps capable of overcoming some of the problems discussed by Louw.

Colin Cameron's chapter, *The Second Betrayal? Commemorating the 10th Anniversay of the Rwandan Genocide,* examines some possible implications of Gilbert's concerns. That is, how to create a new nation out of the horrors of a recent genocide. Rwanda's existence on the global stage is defined by the 1994 genocide, where over 800,000 people were killed. This human tragedy was a result of international betrayal and local conflicts. Much academic and journalistic discourse has been produced analyzing these facts as they unfolded during the genocide and since. However, privileging this genocide as a defining moment ignores all other Rwanda history, limiting Rwanda's location on the world map to a place of human atrocity. Cameron argues that there is a danger of this betrayal being repeated should the international community fail to remember the genocide and instead allow these atrocities to be forgotten. The plans to commemorate the 10th Anniversary of the genocide in Rwanda however, have seen many historical facts whitewashed or forgotten. The current government in Rwanda in its attempt to define a new national identity, has promoted a 'politically correct' view of the genocide which removes any responsibility and culpability from the Rwandan Patriotic Front. Without considering the shattered identities and experiences of that 'defining' national experience, both individual and national identity will remain fragile and thus temporary.

In her chapter entitled *Global Impulses / Local Politics: Comparing Two Eras of Constitution Making in Kenya*, Edith Miguda demonstrates that not all is horrific on the African continent. She suggests that current '*global impulses*' and the local context within Kenya may signal an era of '*post-ethnicity*'', demonstrated by that country's changing Constitution. The global and local context has changed since the first Kenyan Constitution was designed during the decolonisation and independence period, when ethnicity was central to Constitution making. Today it would appear that under an international discourse of human rights and a local discourse on civil society, ethnic cleavages have been weakened, reducing the role of ethnicity in shaping Kenya's revised Constitution. In the present context different cleavages exist that cross ethnic divides, in part a change effected by the impact of globalisation on Kenya. Miguda's chapter contributes a link between the legacies of the colonial period and the current era of globalisation. The chapters then turn to the key political and economic dimensions of globalisation in the context of the dominant discourses of neoliberalism and the War on Terror.

Teresa Thorp, in her chapter, *Economic Partnership Agreements: Reducing Poverty through Enhancing Regional Integration Between the ACP and the EU*, explores whether the complex web of regional trade agreements can foster economic and social integration or whether they will impede the African, Caribbean and Pacific States partner countries on their path to development. Her analysis places lesser developed African countries on the margins of globalisation, with opportunities for development arising from free trade interactions on the global stage, monitored by the rules of the World Trade Organisation. Thorp examines the 2000 Cotonou Agreement, which clearly sets out its aims to eradicate poverty and to integrate the African, Caribbean and Pacific States partners into the global economy through Economic Partnership Agreements. She debates whether this global integration can best be achieved through intra-regional or inter-regional agreements, and whether regional integration itself is more likely to create a sustained change in the peripheral location of these lesser developed countries on the world stage. Thorp argues that regional integration needs to be given greater weight on the global trade agenda but in doing so that a coordinated and dynamic roadmap must ensure success on 3 fronts: intra-regional trade, inter-regional trade, and global integration. Thorp's arguments are not, however, unproblematic and she mentions that one of the challenges for the multilateral institutions involved will be their ability to integrate the informal and private sectors of these countries.

In response to optimistic perspectives on free trade policies, Helen Ware addresses perhaps the key challenge for globalisation in her examination of *The World Bank and African Poverty*. She argues that most Poverty Reduction Programs are based on a model that assumes economic growth will reduce poverty. This model, she argues, ignores the global context. Using case studies from Uganda and Zambia, Ware demonstrates that the problem with these programs lies precisely in the juxtapositioning of neo-liberalism with development. Ware details how the 'growth equals reduced poverty' premise that is central to the Washington Consensus and underpins World Bank and IMF poverty reduction strategies, ensures that the focus of such strategies is on such macro-level concerns as growth and generating fiscal surpluses and by extension, ensuring debt servicing. Such a focus, she argues, establishes an overriding framework that in itself limits the capacity of African states to concentrate on poverty reduction. Similarly, the overarching neo-liberal scaffolding of the Poverty Reduction Strategy Programs renders civil society participation to the margins while simultaneously doing nothing to enhance state-society political linkages which might strengthen democratic institutions in Africa. Ware also illustrates how poverty reduction programs fail to come to terms with the complexity of African development in her examination of the programs in Zambia and Uganda as well as of such key issues as AIDs, education, health and civil conflicts. In the end, Ware concludes that while Poverty Reduction Strategy Program documents provide data which would be useful, their ability to address poverty within Africa will always be limited by the macro-level priorities of neo-liberalism - all the more so, in the context of a globalisation based on Western trade barriers and unfair trade - which are the real issues restricting opportunities for Africa's poor.

The failure of dominant neo-liberal policies to reduce poverty in Africa are seen in their extreme in the cases and issues tackled by William Reno in his chapter on *African Resistance, Colonialism and Contemporary Intervention.* In particular, Reno considers how the global community has responded to those collapsed states since the recent War on Terror began after the 11 September 2001 terrorist attacks on the USA. He argues that the international community has failed in its many attempts to solve the crisis of collapsed states in Africa. Reno questions the local and global forces that contribute to these state collapses and examines why Western strategies that remain based on the prerequisites of democracy and good governance are doomed to failure.

Since 9/11 the Western world has become increasingly concerned with how developing countries control their sovereign territory and 'regulate transactions and movements across borders'. This can be seen as the direct result of attempts to track down terrorist networks revolving around Al Quaida. The US-led 'War on Terror' had its origins in Africa, beginning as far back as 1992 when 'Operation Restore Hope' in Somalia exemplified a dismal lack of understanding by the West of local conflicts in Africa. Subsequent bombings of the US embassies in Nairobi and Dar es Salaam in 1998 precipitated Africa's positioning on the global stage, vis-à-vis the War on Terror. It was immediately decided that no African could have organised nor carried out these destructive attacks on US interests, and thus the hunt for Bin Laden and his associates intensified.

However, since September 2001 there has been a growing recognition of the role of collapsed states in the African region in promulgating regional and international insecurity, therefore justifying a renewed Western involvement in Africa. Reno's chapter assesses this involvement in relation to the local and global forces that result in the collapse and failure of some African states. Reno offers a gloomy prognosis for any African state under the influence of various foreign interventions that reek of 'recolonisation'. Africa's place in the global system of states and the world economy can be seen by the international sanctions preventing 'conflict diamonds' from entering legitimate markets. Reno argues that such strategies, while offering a theory of conflict prevention that includes rebuilding or building up the necessary institutions for democracy and good governance, are doomed to failure in many African states. He argues that democratisation, good governance and economic liberalisation policies, designed to eventually hand control back to African leaders, require the dismantling of rather entrenched 'Shadow State' political economies in order to limit local elites' access to personal power and wealth. This, he argues, will not happen in some cases. But with any map of Africa on the global stage the discerning critic will see that there are 54 African states and not all fail this process. Some have visibly succeeded - and in some sectors Africa does work (see Chabal and Daloz, 1999). The question is how? While answering this question might provide insights for solving the problems of collapsed states, this requires *patience.* Globalisation however, is characterized by a certain urgent impatience.

The *impatience* of the West is demonstrated by Reno's analysis. Wanting to reconstruct failed states as a defence against terrorism reinforces the imposition of so-called solutions to African development, whether influenced by 'global impulses' or local African elites, or more likely both. What results is a cycle of processes that weaken and/or close the spaces for a process of building the nation from the grassroots. For example, the directions taken in post-independence Kenya, led clearly from the top (Western influences and local elites) ensured that any cleavages would be around ethnicity (see Edith Miguda's chapter). This simultaneously encouraged the impatience of policy makers and reinforced some of the difficulties of development. The impatience to 'get things done' results in formations that make it harder to achieve development. After all, we could ask ourselves where was Latin America after 50 years of independence? We cannot completely direct social change. We can have an influence, but we cannot completely control it. In Africa we see the impact of globalisation where 'global impulses' and local forces have tried to direct the systems that undermine the processes from below. Impatience allows no time or space to come to terms with, and deal with, those threats to identity that are caused by rapid social and economic changes. No time or space is allowed by global forces or African elites for Africans to define their own identities and their own development strategies so that the contradictions and tensions thereby created contribute to the undermining of the very development strategies *for* Africa. (see Jane Gilbert and Colin Cameron). Just as Cheru (2002) argues, there is no simple solution, African development will not be achieved by simply focusing on the debate between state-led or market-driven development. The local context of each state must be considered.

Perhaps this is also seen in the exclusions involved in poverty reduction programs and the rebuilding of states under good governance and neo-liberal perspectives which seek to define what is appropriate development and how to achieve it in ways that impose Western versions of 'democratic' identity, forms of states structures, and suitable types of state-society linkages. This process denies Africans the opportunity to build these themselves and perhaps the opportunity for us to appreciate the achievements of those states that have not collapsed. Perhaps it is this very exclusion from the development process that creates the ethnic, religious or political patronage-based cleavages that might result in failed states, and make their successful reconstruction so difficult. If development is about catching up with the West, then with globalisation intensifying everything, it is now all about catching up faster, without allowing any time to understand the complexities of those processes, or indeed the complexities of Africa. This book hopes to shed some light on these complexities and the current attempts "to get Africa to catch up" in the development and globalisation race.

References

Annan, K. (1998) *Report of the UN Secretary General to the Security Council on Africa,* New York, United Nations.

Chabal, P. & Daloz, J. (1999) *Africa Works: Disorder as Political Instrument,* London, James Currey.

Cheru, F. (2002) *African Renaissance: Roadmaps to the Challenge of Globalization,* London and New York, Zed Books; Cape Town, David Philip.

De Waal, A. (2002) "What's New in the New Partnership for Africa's Development", *International Affairs,* 78(3), pp.463-75.

Lyons, T. (2002) "Africa at the 'Edge' of Globalisation," *The Australasian Review of African Studies,* 24(2), pp.38-48.

Pieterse, J. N. (2000) "After Post-Development", *Third World Quarterly*, 21(2), pp.175-191.

Chapter 2

The Impact of Theories of Civilization and Savagery on Native Policy in Colonial Natal

Jeremy Martens

A year before his death, Sir Theophilus Shepstone engaged himself in a debate with Orange Free State President F.W. Reitz over 'native' policy in southern Africa. Reitz had proposed that indirect rule in Natal, with its recognition of native law and chiefly rule, should be abolished. Shepstone, Natal's first Secretary for Native Affairs, responded with a pithy defence of the system of government he had implemented and which bore his name:

> I hold that so long as the social condition of the natives is what it is chieftainship and tribalism are necessary. They are necessary to give us proper control of them, and proper control they must have. I do not believe in the efficacy of violent measures to destroy prejudices; to efface barbarism, or to commend civilised ideas and habits to a barbarous race....Their ancient institutions may be faulty, but they are efficient,

> and can be made so for the purposes of enlightened government ....Civilisation will undermine them by the gradual but sure process of enforcing the fitness of things (Williams 1997: 160).

Shepstone was not alone in asserting that societies should be understood through the lens of civilization and barbarism, for similar views shaped settler perceptions of Africans, rationalized white supremacy, guided policy decisions and informed legislation throughout colonial South Africa (see Bank 1995;1997; and Elbourne 1999).

This paper briefly examines the impact of theories of civilization and barbarism on the form of rule adopted in colonial Natal. Such an examination is important, for the significance of these theories extended beyond the colony's borders. While 19th century settlers did not think in terms of 'Zuluness' their assertion that all Africans in KwaZulu-Natal shared a homogeneous barbaric culture and society blinded them to the complex kinship identities that existed in south east Africa. This characterization foreshadowed white constructions of the Zulu in the 20th century.

For much of the 19th century, British attitudes towards colonization were informed by a stadial theory of societal development (Maloney 2001). Principally derived from the writings of influential Scottish Enlightenment thinkers, this theory posited that humankind was comprised of a diverse variety of peoples at different developmental stages. All societies occupied a place on the scale between savagery and civilization; at the bottom of the scale were the 'rude' savage tribes of America and Australia, at the top the civilized 'polished nations' of Europe. While this formulation rested upon an assumption of European supremacy, it was distinct from biologically racist theories of the late nineteenth and early twentieth centuries. Enlightenment philosophers rejected the idea that there were innate differences between the savage and civilized; for them, all people regardless of origin belonged to a single human family and inherited a universal human nature. Human differentiation resulted from environmental conditions, especially the state of societies in which people lived.

According to Enlightenment theory, all societies naturally passed through four economic stages, each phase corresponding to a different mode of subsistence. Hunting communities gradually evolved into pastoral societies, which, over time, developed agriculture. Eventually, agricultural communities made the final progression to commercial society, the apogee of human organization. Moreover, it was argued that as the mode of subsistence varied in societies, so too did customs, manners and morals, as well as ideas and institutions relating to law, property and government (eg Meek 1976: 2).

Because it asserted that all human societies evolved similarly, the four stages theory ignored differences between communities regarded as uncivilized. Thus, pastoral societies in different parts of the world were often assumed to share similar laws, morals and customs. When translated to the colonial context, this assumption encouraged educated administrators to approach the governance of colonized peoples in certain prescribed ways. This investigation will concentrate on those Enlightenment ideas relating to chieftainship, governance and the position of women in savage societies, and the extent to which they influenced native policy in colonial Natal.

Chieftainship in Early Colonial Natal

When explaining the development of indirect rule in colonial Natal, historians emphasise a number of factors: the strength of Nguni institutions; the unwillingness of the British to spend large sums of money on African administration; the pragmatic genius of Theophilus Shepstone; and the practical necessity of cultivating indigenous allies to safeguard colonial security (see Welsh 1971; Etherington 1989; Guy 1997). The validity of these factors is beyond dispute, nevertheless, it is possible that ideas about civilization and savagery played a more significant role in shaping the Shepstone system than has hitherto been acknowledged. British preconceptions about the indigenous inhabitants of Natal were in no small measure influenced by Enlightenment theories about appropriate forms of government for savage societies.

Adam Ferguson (1966: 100-105), John Millar (1779: 171-197) and others had argued in the late 18th century that "the uniform history of mankind in a barbarous state" demonstrated that when "rude nations" made the transition from hunters to herders and farmers, their mode of government changed to reflect evolving distinctions between "the leader and follower, the prince and the subject". Chiefs emerged to lead large communities, but resorted to "the bridle of despotism and military force" to control their followers' "warlike and turbulent spirit". Consequently, "[r]apacity and terror" became the "predominant motives of conduct", forming "the character of the only parties into which mankind are divided, that of the oppressor, and that of the oppressed". In this state, the power of superstition led to the creation of an "order of men" who used magic and who sometimes gave communities "an early taste of despotism and absolute slavery". Over time chiefs asserted control over land and assumed legislative power. And, once members of the tribe were dependent on him with regard to their property, they were "in no condition to dispute his commands, or to refuse obedience to those ordinances which he issues at pleasure" (Ferguson 1966: 100-105; Millar 1779: 171-197).

The 1847 Locations Commission Report was one of the first documents to outline the principles of Natal native administration, and its assertion that prosperity depended on "management and efficient control of the large native population" guided colonial policy into the 20th century. The recommendation that locations be set aside for African habitation, the administration of law involve "chiefs and councillors" and legal decisions be adapted as much as possible "to the usages and customs of the native law" were predicated on a understanding of society very similar to that of Ferguson and Millar. Africans' "universal character" was "superstitious and warlike", they had a low regard for human life, and their passions were "easily enflamed". These characteristics were not innate, however, but were formed by "education, habits and associations". Africans had "grown up in habits of such servile compliance to the wills of their despotic rulers, that they still show ready obedience to constituted authority" (Locations Commission Report 1848: 132).

Earl Grey (1848), Secretary of State for the Colonies, endorsed the Commission's assessment of African society. "It is obvious", he asserted, "that those who have hitherto been under a rule of despotic severity cannot without extreme danger be emancipated from all control". It was therefore essential that the Natal government abstain "from any sudden or violent interference with the authority exercised over these people by their own chiefs". Africans should continue to "administer justice towards each other as they had been used to do in former times", although chiefs should be restrained from "those acts of cruelty and tyranny which are so common among savages". However, this restraint should be sparingly exercised so that chiefly power was not diminished and the chiefs were not "lowered in the eyes of their tribes", for their:

> maintaining a strong authority affords the only means by which in the actual state of things ab-

> solute anarchy and confusion can be averted, and it would therefore be advisable to abstain from examining too minutely into the manner in which the chiefs may rule over their tribes, even though this should unfortunately allow of the existence of much oppression, and the commission of many acts highly repugnant to our notions of justice and humanity (Grey 1848: 138-9).

These principles of government were embodied in the Royal Instructions of 1848 that recognized the validity of customary law and the powers which "the laws, customs, and usages of the inhabitants" had vested in the chiefs. These principles also underpinned the enactment of Ordinance 3 of 1849, which gave to the Lieutenant Governor "all the power and authority which, according to the laws, customs, and usages of the natives, are held and enjoyed by any supreme or paramount native chief"(Cited in Welsh 1971: 14,17). Indirect rule in Natal therefore fitted neatly within the theory that savage societies were suited to despotic rule, and that any tampering with this rule would result in anarchy. An enlightened, 'decentralized despotism' (Mamdami 1996) was the best that civilized government could provide. That Theophilus Shepstone shared these ideas for the whole of his career is evidenced by the quotation at the beginning of this chapter.

If the transition from barbarism to civilization was a gradual process, enlightened government could at least facilitate the process through the encouragement of "industry and the formation of a taste for the comforts and luxuries of civilized life" (Grey 1848: 223). Ferguson (1966: 101; Millar 1779: 43) had argued that in between

> the prospects of ruin and conquest the barbarian spent every moment of relaxation in the in-

> dulgence of sloth. He cannot descend to the pursuits of industry or mechanical labour.

Earl Grey (1848: 222) applied a similar formula to the "Zoolahs located in Natal". He agreed with Harry Smith's (1848: 218) assessment that Africans in the colony had inherited "that apathetic idea of comfort comprised in having a sufficiency to eat and time to sleep", arguing that this disposition was one "which almost universally distinguishes uncivilized men" (Grey 1848: 222).

The imposition of a system of taxation would not only increase the revenue of the colony, and provide funds for schools and other beneficial institutions, but would also encourage Africans to "acquire habits of industry" and raise them in the scale of civilisation (Grey 1848: 222). The form of taxation eventually adopted was a "rate upon their huts", fixed at 7s per annum. Shepstone argued a hut tax was the most just to impose, for it embraced "every advantage of both a property and an income tax, and has the further recommendation of directly discouraging poligamy [sic], that great incentive to the exclusive acquirement of cattle, as the most desirable description of property" (Shepstone 1850: 65). The adoption of the hut tax was a seminal moment in Natal's development of indirect rule, and the connections Shepstone drew between taxation, polygamy and civilization would continue to shape revenue collection in the colony.

Colonial Debates over African Marriage

The issue of African marriage was central to settler discussions about civilization and barbarism. As early as 1847, the Locations Commission had insisted that any "improvement of the natives" depended on "raising their women in the scale of native society", for "polygamy and bartering for women prevail universally in their worst form in the district" (Locations Commission Report 1848: 133). No official action was taken until 1869, when regulations proclaimed under a new law imposed a tax on every marriage contracted by Africans, restricted the practice of *lobola* (bride price) and required that brides publicly express their assent before an official witness for marriages to be valid. The implementation of these measures unleashed a storm of protest from white settlers and missionaries (Welsh 1971: 67-96; Martens 2001: 78-134).

While economic considerations informed both the government's decision to pass the 1869 legislation and settlers' opposition to the law, both sides drew from ideas of civilisation and savagery to defend their positions. In Enlightenment theory, the condition of women was regarded as an index of the level of civilization of any society. It was argued that among savages "the women of a family are usually treated as the servants or slaves of the men" and that nothing could exceed the "dependence and subjection in which they are kept, or the toil and drudgery which they are obliged to undergo" (Millar 1779: 42-43). Wives in these societies were "bought and sold, like any other species of property" by their husbands from their fathers and "the conclusion of a bargain of this nature, together with the payment of the price, has therefore become the most usual form of solemnity in the celebration of their marriages" (Millar 1779: 49). This theory helps explain why white Natalians frequently compared African polygamous marriages to slavery transactions. African men supposedly purchased large numbers of African women and regarded them as property, to be bought and sold like cattle. Black women were little more than drudges, forced to slave in the fields while their men folk sat idle. It was lamented that this savagery resulted in downtrodden women and unmanly, promiscuous, lazy men.

While all white Natalians agreed that female oppression was a sign of African barbarism, they could not agree on the best way to ameliorate the position of women and thereby raise African society in the scale of civilisation. Settlers and missionaries argued that moral legislation abolishing traditional African marriage practices would allow civilised domestic relations to emerge, and consequently, black women and men would be rescued from barbarism. Conveniently, the enforcement of civilised monogamous marriages would also encourage black men to work for whites. Officials in contrast insisted that the only judicious way to facilitate civilization was to employ indirect methods to regulate African marriage practices, rather than abolish them outright. Furthermore, officials insisted that the marriage tax would encourage Africans to enter the employ of settlers and augment the treasury.

In 1869, Shepstone (1869: 23) recommended the new marriage regulations on the grounds that their implementation could "only favour the operation of natural causes to achieve the extinction of polygamy". And, when called upon to defend the law, he reported that its provisions had the effect of "protecting the young suitor from the mere property competition of the rich old polygamist: - in short, it makes the union a marriage, instead of practically a mere sale". He went on to state that the application of the law since 1869 had greatly improved "[i]n every respect...the condition of both the young men and women...and native marriage has been placed on a better footing" (Shepstone 1875: 125).

Lieutenant Governor Keate (1868: 321) endorsed Shepstone's appraisal of the measure. As far as he was concerned, African marriages were a form of payment or barter as Africans themselves had

> reached a certain stage at which the conditions of their life are such as to render to them, as to the patriarchs of old a multitude of wives and children a means towards the possession of wealth in the shape of flocks and herds and cultivated fields.

In African society "at present it is the wives and children who support by their labour the heads of families", and until "surrounding circumstances so change as to throw upon the husband and the father the work and the duty of supporting wife and children polygamy will prevail" (Keate 1868: 321)

Any attempt to tackle polygamy directly would be imprudent, because "all that can be done by legislative interference is to help on and remove obstructions [to] the natural causes which are leading however slowly to that result" (Keate 1868: 321). The means by which the marriage registration measure would help on and remove these 'obstructions' would be by giving

> to the woman, what has hitherto been entirely denied to her, a voice in her own disposal, and by so doing tend to raise her in her own estimation and in the social scale, and thus give her an influence in the control and management of her own family and eventually beyond its limits (Keate 1868: 321).

Furthermore, the marriage tax would serve to increase the supply of African labour to settlers by encouraging "labour habits among the male portion of the native community upon which more than anything else the extinction of polygamy depends" (Keate 1868: 321).

The leading settler opponent of the legislation was *Natal Witness* editor R. E. Ridley. In his editorials, Ridley (1869) detailed how the legal recognition of "a vicious and brutal polygamy" and "woman slavery" condemned Africans to barbarism. If settlers wanted Africans to continue "to be shrouded in the thick mantle of superstition and vice" and to remain impervious to Christianity and "the gentle teaching of civilization", then they should strengthen and foster Africans in their "present depravity". If, however, white Natalians had

> any faith that this tractable savage can be raised, can be weaned from his brutalizing customs, can learn the practices of civilization, and can appreciate the high truths and discharge the holy duties of our common Christianity, then let us cancel this foolish law (Ridley 1869).

Legalising polygamy, Ridley (1869) maintained, had the effect of "making the savage habits of the Kafir perpetual".

Ridley explained to his readers that the law made "the custom whereby Kafir men transfer the women, as property, from one to another" an "authorized institution, the sale and price of women having been proclaimed as law" (Ridley 1869). In the minds of colonists, this barbaric slavery hindered the establishment of a civilised commercial society in Natal. Well known settler, Thomas Phipson argued that if it were not for the savage state of African society, the white settler "would be able to sell his labour or produce in a fair market" and would be able to afford "the food and clothing appertaining to civilized life" (Cited in Currey 1968: 131). Good prices would be obtained for agricultural products on one hand, and "consumers, employed in arts, trades and commerce", would be found on the other. However, as things stood, none of these things could happen because

> [t]he black man either sets to work the girls and women whom he breeds or buys, or he '*sebenzas*' (for work it cannot properly be called) a few months for the white man, and spends his money in cattle and women; or lastly, he ploughs himself (or makes his boys do it more likely), and thus comes into the market as a competitor with his civilized neighbour (Currey 1968: 131-2).

Although Phipson claimed that Africans had a right to live "barbarously, to wear rags, or skins, or nothing, when at home, to eschew groceries and squat in a beehive hut", by doing so they tended "to drag down to the same level" all who competed with them in agriculture. The settler farmer could not afford to live a civilised life "so long as his savage competitor continues to be a savage, and so to undersell him" (Currey 1968: 132).

Settler opposition to the marriage legislation was too powerful to ignore, and consequently the Natal government abolished the marriage tax in 1875. Even so, the fact that both settlers and officials employed Enlightenment theories about civilization and savagery to defend their respective positions indicates the significance of these ideas to policy formulation in colonial Natal.

CONCLUSION

Debates about African barbarism and European civilization were ubiquitous in colonial Natal. From the vantage point of the 21st century, it is easy to dismiss these debates as crude settler racism. However, the importance of Enlightenment theories of societal development should not be underestimated, for they helped shape Natal's system of indirect rule and informed legislation affecting Africans, the legacy of which continues to influence political developments in contemporary KwaZulu-Natal. Furthermore, these theories encouraged settlers to ignore the historical and cultural diversity of the African inhabitants of Natal. This erasure of difference strongly resembles later characterisations of the Zulu by whites in the 20th century.

References

Bank, A. (1995) 'Liberals and Their Enemies: Racial Ideology at the Cape of Good Hope, 1820 to 1850', Unpublished Ph.D. dissertation, University of Cambridge.

Bank, A. (1997) 'The Great Debate and the Origins of South African Historiography', *Journal of African History,* 38, pp. 261-281.

Currey, R. (ed.) (1968), *Letters & Other Writings of a Natal Sheriff: Thomas Phipson 1815-76,* Cape Town.

Elbourne, E. (1999) 'Domesticity and Dispossession: the Ideology of "Home" and the British Construction of the "Primitive" From the Eighteenth to the Early Nineteenth Centuries', Unpublished paper, Princeton.

Etherington, N. (1989) 'The "Shepstone System" in the Colony of Natal and beyond the borders' in A. Duminy and B. Guest (eds), *Natal and Zululand from Earliest Times to 1910: A New History,* Pietermaritzburg, pp. 170-192.

Ferguson, A. (1966) *An Essay on the History of Civil Society 1767,* Reprint, Edinburgh University Press.

Grey, E. to Smith, H. 10 December 1847 in BPP British Parliamentary Papers (1848) *Correspondence Relative to the Establishment of the Settlement of Natal* Presented July 1848, London.

Guy, J. (1997) 'An Accommodation of Patriarchs: Theophilus Shepstone and the Foundations of the System of Native Administration in Natal', Unpublished paper, Durban.

Keate to Buckingham and Chandos, 24 October 1868 in Pietermaritzburg Archives Repository Government House Files (1868) 1216, pp. 313-329.

Locations Commission Report in British Parliamentary Papers (1848) *Correspondence Relative to the Establishment of the Settlement of Natal* Presented July 1848, London.

Maloney, P. (2001) 'Savagery and Civilization: Early Victorian Notions', *New Zealand Journal of History*, 35(2), pp.153-4.

Mamdani, M. (1996) *Citizen and Subject: Contemporary Africa and the Legacy of Late Colonialism,* Princeton University Press.

Martens, J. (2001) 'So Destructive of Domestic Security and Comfort': Settler Domesticity, Race and the Regulation of African Behaviour in the Colony of Natal, 1843-1893', Unpublished Ph.D. thesis, Queen's University at Kingston.

Meek, R. (1976) *Social Science and the Ignoble Savage*, Cambridge University Press, Cambridge and New York.

Millar, J. (1779) *The Origin of the Distinction of Ranks; or An Inquiry into the Circumstances which give Rise to Influence and Authority in the Different Members of Society,* 3rd Edition, London.

Ridley, E.R. (1869) *Natal Witness,* 11 May 1869.

Shepstone, T. (1850), 'Memorandum on Hut Tax, 18 June 1849' in British Parliamentary Papers *Correspondence Relating to the Settlement of Natal,* Presented August 1850, London.

Shepstone, T. (1869) 'Memorandum: Registration of Native Marriages', 22 March in Pietermaritzburg Archives Repository, Secretary for Native Affairs Files 1/7/8, pp.18-23.

Shepstone, T. (1875) 'Memorandum on the Law No 1, 1869', 5 January in Pietermaritzburg Archives Repository, Secretary for Native Affairs Files 1/7/7, pp. 122-129.

Smith, H. to Grey, E., 4 March 1848, in BPP British Parliamentary Papers (1848) *Correspondence Relative to the Establishment of the Settlement of Natal,* Presented July 1848, London.

Welsh, D. (1971) *The Roots of Segregation: Native Policy in Colonial Natal,* Oxford University Press, Cape Town and New York.

Williams, J.A. (1997) *From the South African Past: Narratives, Documents and Debates,* Boston and New York, Houghton Mifflin.

Chapter 3

Afrikaner and South African Black Nationalism: A Cultural Studies Perspective.

Eric Louw

Cultural Studies is concerned with the relationship between power and culture. For Stuart Hall (1977) national identity would be regarded as the outcome of a process of contextually-bound semiosis, and nations viewed as linguistic representations, arising as people relate to each other within a matrix of power-relations. From this point of view we continually construct, and reconstruct, ourselves as we live our lives; attaching ourselves to the available, discursively constructed, 'subject-positions'. Hall's method provides a way of conceptualizing nation-building projects as a set of relationships between ethnicity, class and power; relationships rooted in particular contexts. It foregrounds the way 'beliefs' and identity-construction are shaped by our historical material contexts, existent power-relations, and narratives from the past. These beliefs/identities/narratives then shape contemporary political behaviour, policy-formations, and the next round of identity-formation etcetera. Cultural Studies provides a method for examining this identity-construction and hence the identities and cultures underpinning Africa's political processes. In short, Cultural Studies provides another perspective on nation building from the perspective of the (contextually-bound) ideologies, narratives and discourses that people use to construct their identities and guide their behaviours.

CONSTRUCTING IDENTITY

Individuals are 'made social' (socialized) by having linguistically-constructed 'pictures' put into their heads. Wilhelm Dilthey's notion of a 'worldview' (*Weltanschauung*) encapsulates how people come to 'see' the world through acquiring knowledge, beliefs and language. A *Weltanschauung* provides an individual with a fulcrum around which to construct a 'map' for guiding his/her life. A worldview mixes 'belief' (rational and emotional) and 'lived experience' (action-in-the-world) – a mix of discourse and practice. Over the years, many concepts have been developed to describe the phenomenon of how people 'see' the world' and 'act' in accordance with these visions. Hall (1977: 330) used the term "maps of meaning"; Rokeach (1960: 18-19) referred to "belief systems"; George (1969) called them "operational codes"; and Boulding (1956) said people develop "an image" of the world. Dilthey's "*Weltanschauung*" or worldview encapsulates all of these.

So where do worldviews come from? What is the mechanism by which political socialization takes place? Effectively, humans become embedded within sets of discourses and practices. Each individual is born into a context where pre-existing meanings and practices exists; these are internalized as individuals imbibe and absorb the signs, codes and practices of their social environment. Hence, the discourses and practices of liberal democracy are now simply taken for granted in places like the United States and Australia. At heart, socialization is the acquisition of language as mediated by the family, media and schooling. The socialization process positions individuals into sets of social relationships, some of which are political. Thus, the acquisition of political worldviews is related to the process of interpellation (Althusser, 1971: 162-163). Humans are embedded into, and embed themselves into, belief systems as they interact with their linguistic environment. We come to 'know' who we 'are' because our identities (who we think we are) and status are embedded within representational systems; we are positioned within a system of language.

Effectively, acquiring worldviews is the acquisition of ideology. By internalizing representations around us (especially in the media and school), we embed ourselves into those 'pictures of the world' made available to us. Hence, ideology is not imposed upon us. Rather, we actively participate in interpellating ourselves through engaging with our cultural environment. For Althusserians, ideology is a system of *coding* reality with ideology emerging from a system of signification (signs and codes) (See Heck, 1980). This Althusserian conceptualization of ideology emphasizes the 'subjective' dimension of socialization; that is the language (signs and codes) we internalize provides us with the material from which to construct our 'visions' of the world, and of our relationship to this world. This constitutes the mechanism for positioning citizens into sets of 'imaginary lived relations' (Hall, 1977: 329). But ideology is not merely 'subjective'. It also has an 'objective' dimension, in that we also learn to interact with a material world by learning practices, such as the 'appropriate' use of cultural objects (furniture, work-place tools, roads, 'private property', etcetera). Volosinov (1973) pointed to ideology's dual subjective-objective dimension. Deploying Volosinov offers a semiotic approach to ideological-analysis (see Louw & Tomaselli: 1991) that corrects the Althusserians overly subjectivist view.

Worldviews are a curious phenomenon. Each individual actively constructs his/her own worldview through a process of engaging with and drawing upon linguistic material in his/her environment. Individuals actively construct their own worldviews using pre-existing discourses and practices as 'representational resources'. Thus, worldviews are not predetermined or static. Humans are not encoded-automatons, trapped inside a 'prison house of language' because humans are capable of struggling over the encoding possibilities of meaning. However, worldviews are significantly 'guided' by existing 'pools of meaning' and encoding rules. In all societies, it is possible to identify a pool of meaning that has become hegemonically dominant at any point in time, e.g. liberal-secularism is dominant in contemporary US, British and Australian society. Because existing signification systems are the raw material from which individuals construct worldviews, the scope to influence people is great; that is people can be steered by manipulating the available encoding possibilities. Effectively, those staffing key meaning-making sites (like media and schools) are worldview 'agenda setters', because they influence the pool of signs and codes from which the next wave of worldviews will be constructed. Not surprisingly, ruling elites pay considerable attention to this agenda setting function.

USING CULTURAL STUDIES TO DECONSTRUCT SOUTH AFRICAN POLITICAL BEHAVIOUR

Gavin Kitching (2000) suggests African Studies has not been up to the task of explaining what was happening in Africa and why it is happening. Perhaps one reason is that African Studies scholars have failed to get 'into the heads' of Africans and examine the discourses and narratives underpinning their identity-constructions (and hence, their behaviours).

Cultural Studies provides a method for examining the

identities and cultures underpinning Africa's political processes and attempts (successful and failed) at nation building. Cultural Studies directs us to focus on:

- How ideologies, narratives and discourses are constructed (by intellectuals) and circulated (by teachers and journalists, etcetera).
- How ideas/worldviews (in the form of textuality and intertextuality) are encoded and decoded within specific contextual frameworks and power-relationships.
- How these ideas/worldviews underpin ruling elites and the hegemonies that these elites construct.
- The relationship between ideologies, narratives and discourses and the building (and maintenance) of concrete infrastructures (e.g. economies, patronage-networks, service-delivery, etcetera).

This Cultural Studies approach can be applied to South Africa to deconstruct the contextually-bounded worldviews and behaviours of those political actors who shaped the 3 models of nation building and modernization that characterized 20th century South Africa: Anglo settler-capitalism; Afrikaner nationalism; and black nationalism.

The Milner Model of Settler Capitalism

After the Boer War, Lord Milner and his 'kindergarten' were responsible for the post-war reconstruction of South Africa (Nimocks 1968). Milner's kindergarten was a small tight-knit group of Oxford University graduates, drawn from the heart of the Anglo-establishment, who were committed to the task of Empire-building. They were sent out to Africa to build British hegemony. This 'kindergarten' effectively created the basic political-economic outlines of a new modern state of South Africa. The Milner model, which has underpinned the South African social formation ever since, encoded the dominant discourses and narratives underpinning British colonialism. Milner's own notes and correspondence are infused with this British colonial and imperial discourse (Headlam, 1933).

Milner's kindergarten laid the foundations for a British Southern African hegemony by:

- Creating the conditions for a new modern state. South Africa and South African-ness thereafter emerged within the boundaries of a new administrative entity; which conveniently served the needs of a modern (Anglo-dominated) capitalist economy (that necessarily also served the Empire's economic interests). The kindergarten modernity, in the form of Anglo-liberal capitalism, represented 'progress' over the lower forms of socio-economic organization represented by Afrikaners and black-Africans.
- Constructing a new civil service, police, judiciary and local government infrastructure as a fulcrum within which modern capitalism could grow. Anglo settlers were imported for the purpose of staffing these new infrastructures.
- Laying the foundations for South Africa's 20th century labour arrangements.
- Constructing a new framework for an integrated Southern African capitalist economy, with Witwatersrand gold-mining lying at the centre of this new economic-order.
- Dividing the country into areas for white settlement and black reserves.
- Building an education and media infrastructure that serviced the needs of Britain's hegemony over South Africa; that is Anglo cultural hegemony was entrenched. Anglo teachers and educational-administrators were imported for the purpose of circulating discourses ap-

propriate to the needs of British hegemony and Anglo dominated capitalism.

- Laying the foundations for a racial-capitalist state, such as a socio-economic order grounded in a state-sanctioned class-race hierarchy.
- Entrenching white supremacy.

However, Milner never succeeded in fully implementing his original model of British hegemony, primarily because he was unable to attract enough Anglo settlers to South Africa to achieve a fully-fledged Anglo-settler society of the Australian type. Instead, the kindergarten restructured the original Milner model so as to rely upon 'moderate' Afrikaners administering the new British dominion. This involved converting Afrikaner leaders like Louis Botha and Jan Smuts to Anglo discourses and practices. These leaders built the Anglo-Afrikaner alliance-politics that ultimately serviced the needs of Anglo mining-capital (constituting the economic heart of British hegemony over Southern Africa).

The three most significant effects of the establishment of early 20th century Anglo hegemony over Southern Africa were: first, the creation of a new modernizing state; and second, the reconfiguration of the socio-economic order in accordance with the (modernizing) principles of racial-capitalism. Thirdly, associated with this reordering was the naturalization of an ethnic-ranking discourse that underpinned the modernizing-capitalist project of 20th century South Africa. This ethnic-ranking discourse had profound repercussions in 20th century South Africa, because its spawning of the 'catch-up nationalisms' of Afrikaner and South African black nationalism.

A feature of the British Empire was an ethnic-ranking system that Donald Horowitz (1985: 184) has called 'positional psychology'. In other words, ethnic ranking allocated group worth. Within the colonial system there were what

Horowitz called 'backward' and advanced' groups. One's worth as an individual was ascribed according to the ethnic group one was born into. An Empire-wide colonial ethnic-ranking system existed as a worldview that justified English-rule over an Empire of lesser human-types. A unified British South Africa was established in 1910 as a white oligarchy in which Anglos were dominant. Racial oligarchy was encoded into South Africa's very origins as a unified capitalist state and has remained a feature of the South African state ever since. As Horowitz (1985: 154) said:

> the colonialists thus set in motion a comparative process by which aptitudes and disabilities imputed to ethnic groups were to be evaluated ... [and] the evaluations took hold ...[so that] ... no one emerged from colonial rule untouched by the new standards of group evaluation.

To be born a white Anglo was to see oneself, and be seen by others, as automatically superior and 'advanced'. To be born a black South African was to be automatically 'backward'. To be born Afrikaans was to be allocated to an intermediary position; not as 'advanced' as Anglos, but not as 'backward' as blacks. Anglos saw Afrikaners as 'honorary Europeans', slightly 'better than blacks', but somehow tainted by their long association with Africa. This, Anglo-manufactured, ascribed ranking affected not only one's economic life chances, but also one's perceived self-worth. It was a social order in which non-Anglos could never feel fully worthy. This produced a sense of inferiority because being in a 'backward' (or intermediary) position produced a feeling of being 'weak and helpless' vis-à-vis the 'advanced' group (Horowitz 1985: 170). It also produced a form of self-stereotyping in which members of the 'backward' groups adopted compliant personalities characterized by unassertiveness, an unambitious demeanour and the assumption that others were more intelligent, better educated and more worthwhile (Horowitz 1985: 170-171). Besides being psychologically unsettling, exclusion from the 'advanced' group produced feelings of envy, insecurity and deprivation (Jesudason 1995: 7). This envy, insecurity and deprivation had profound effects on subsequent socio-political developments in South Africa precisely because it produced 'catch-up nationalisms' amongst Afrikaners and black South Africans. These two catch-up nationalisms (with their policies of apartheid and black empowerment) are attempts by groups psychologically damaged by the Anglo-colonial ranking system to re-arrange the ranking order and so achieve the same recognition accorded to the 'advanced' group (Horowitz, 1985: 165). They are nationalisms triggered by pain.

Ultimately, one of the great unintended consequences of Milner's model was apartheid, which emerged from the profound impact the Milner model had on the Afrikaner psyche. In particular, Milner's policy of attempting to Anglicize Afrikaners by banning the use of Afrikaans in schools had profound consequences. This led to the founding of Afrikaner CNO-schools (*Christelik Nasionale Onderwys*/Christian National Education) organized by parent committees and *dominees* (Calvinist ministers of religion). From these CNO-schools emerged the ideology of 'Christian Nationalism'. And from this grew the Afrikaner nationalist notion of *eiesoortigheid* ('own-ness'), which mutated into apartheid.

Afrikaner Nationalism and Apartheid

Thus, we can view Afrikaner nationalism as a by-product of Milner's post-Boer War reconstruction. This reconstruction turned Johannesburg into a sub-metropole of capitalism. South Africa's formerly agricultural-based, largely pastoral, economy was transformed into a predominantly urban-economy, centred upon mining. Whites in particular were rapidly urbanized as the capitalization of agriculture drove surplus populations into the cities. The urbanization of Afrikaners after the Boer War saw impoverished Afrikaners congregate into shack-land slums. The first quarter of the 20th century saw these working class and lumpenproletariat Afrikaners turn to the South African Communist Party in large numbers. This culminated in the 1922 declaration of a people's republic in Johannesburg/ Witwatersrand (Herd 1966). The military was mobilized to crush this uprising. Ultimately, the struggle between the National Party/NP (led by middle class Afrikaners) and the Communist Party over this Afrikaner constituency left a long-lasting legacy of Afrikaner middle class fear of communism; a legacy that became enmeshed within apartheid.

Milner's modernizing state also created a small urban Afrikaner middle class that experienced not only the dislocation of rapid urbanization (de-pastoralization), but also experienced the trauma of having to function in an Anglicized urban environment. Within Milner's ethnic-ranking structure they found themselves to be second-class citizens. This middle class, especially its intellectuals, *dominees*, teachers and social workers already resentful about Anglicization, came to blame Anglo-capitalism for the impoverishment of their fellow-Afrikaners in the slums, and the rise of communism. The *dominees* were, in particular, concerned about the latter because it was seen to threaten their Christian values. It was the middle class Afrikaners who led the NP; promoting Christian Nationalism as a means for Afrikaners to deliver themselves from the poverty, dislocation, pain and second-class-ness of Anglo-capitalist hegemony (presented as an alternative to the Communists' solutions to Anglo-capitalism).

In this regard, Jesudason (1995: 7) has noted that "deprived individuals and their leaders, especially if they possess strong cultural and affective ties, are prone to using the state to ... modify the opportunity structure of society". The British created the ethnic ranking-system and the pain associated with being ranked badly. Having done this, the conditions were created, in the many multi-ethnic societies created by the British Empire, for one or other ethnic group to seize state power in order to use it for a group-based socio-economic policy of catch-up.

The earliest such nationalist catch-up project was undertaken by the intermediary-ranked Afrikaner nationalists. Apartheid was an enormous ethnic re-ranking and 'affirmative action' project designed by the NP to upgrade Afrikaners who had been impoverished by the British capitalization/modernization of South Africa after the Boer War. This upgrade-program was imbued by the spirit of what has been dubbed *volkskapitalisme*, 'people's capitalism' (O'Meara 1983), which involved building a parallel Afrikaner economy. To achieve this, the NP focused its energy on capturing the state, which was subsequently used as a vehicle to create opportunities for Afrikaner advancement. Afrikaner poverty was to be eliminated not through charity, but by using the state to rearrange opportunity-structures. The result was the creation of an ethnic-patronage system. The NP used its control of the state to dispense patronage to its ethnic constituency. Apartheid became, in effect, a huge affirmative action program for Afrikaners; the NP dispensed public service jobs and built a huge education system of Afrikaner schools, colleges and universities in order to upgrade their constituency. An interesting feature of this Afrikaner affirmative action program was that the NP created *separate* structures alongside and parallel to the Anglo-structures. Initially 'standards' were not as high in the parallel Afrikaner institutions, in that Afrikaners were effectively 'protected' from Anglo competition. However, standards were raised over a twenty-year period until they reached the same level as the Anglo institutions. This parallel infrastructure was paid for by taxing businesses in South Africa, which were generally Anglo-owned. The trade-off for these businesses was, as O'Meara (1983: 247) argues, that the state facilitated the exploitation of black workers by the business-sector. Apartheid meant businesses could, even after paying tax, generate substantive profits (from exploiting black people), and not be 'damaged' by having less competent people forced on them by affirmative action. Hence the Anglo business sector was left unscathed by Afrikaner affirmative action during the up-grade/transition period.

At the heart of the process of creating Afrikaner Nationalism was a group of radical intellectuals (De Klerk, 1975) who successfully fashioned, popularized and naturalized a set of narratives which, by 1948, were able to mobilize and unify a diversity of Afrikaners previously separated by regional and class differences, urban-rural cleavages, and hostilities dating back to the Boer War (when Afrikanerdom was divided between those who capitulated to the British and those who fought to the bitter end). These early Afrikaner nationalists invested considerable energy into building up an Afrikaans-language print media to popularize their ideas. Further, they created an organization (similar to the Masons) called the Broederbond to promote their nationalism and geared to placing as many *Broeders* ('Brothers') as possible into key positions in society. Much effort was expended in winning over teachers and journalists. The career-trajectory of the man often credited with 'inventing' apartheid, Hendrik Verwoerd, reveals much about the way Afrikaner nationalism emerged and grew. Verwoerd was initially a social work professor (concerned about Afrikaner poverty) who then became the founding editor of a newspaper created to promote Afrikaner nationalism in the

Transvaal. Thereafter, he moved into a Parliamentary career.

Effectively, intellectuals like Verwoerd created a new set of 'subject positions' for Afrikaners to occupy. A new identity and/or 'imagined community' (Anderson, 1991) was forged. At its heart, this new identity stressed *eiesoortigheid* (own-ness), a notion based upon the Dutch principle of *verzuiling* (the pillarization of society). Using this 'own-ness' as its justification, the NP demanded the right for Afrikaners to have their own 'cultural space' separate from Anglos and from black South Africans. They convinced their newly mobilized constituency that this was the way to prevent Afrikaners from being 'swamped' by both Anglo cultural imperialism and black majoritarianism. These intellectuals adeptly used the 1938 Voortrekker centenary celebrations to mobilize a sense of 'own-ness' and opposition to Anglo-hegemony. Then, during the Second World War, black migrants began streaming into the cities to staff the new factories producing munitions for Britain. The Afrikaner nationalist intelligentsia was able to use this as further evidence of the need for the NP to gain control of the state in order to create the conditions necessary for 'own-ness, in the sense of 'separate development', and stop this black migration. From this, the notion of apartheid was born.

Early apartheid was constructed around the following nationalist discourses:

1. Afrikaner resistance to Anglicization, that is the notion of *eiesoortigheid* and a language-struggle (Steyn 1987).
2. The NP response to the growth of an Afrikaner working class/ lumpenproletariat: (i) formulating affirmative action for the "volk" (which was offered to Afrikaners as an alternative to communism); (ii) opposing Smuts and the United Party (who represented South African

capitalist interests and Milner's racial-capitalism); and (iii) formulating policies which retained the basic outlines of racial-capitalism, but pushed Afrikaners up the ethnic-class scale. Effectively, although the basic outline of Milner's modernization project was retained, the NP produced a modified modernization and nation building program.

3. Middle class *dominees* within the NP and their concern about the lumpenproletariat Afrikaners living in shackland slums (it is worth noting that the first NP apartheid Prime Minister, D.F. Malan was a *dominee*).
4. The sense of 'minority-ness' that led to a fear black majoritarianism. Much of apartheid was about trying to find mechanisms for geographically delineating 'white South Africa' and keeping blacks out of this white territory.
5. This sense of 'minority-ness' also caused the NP to oppose Anglo migration into South Africa because of a fear of being culturally 'swamped'.
6. Afrikaner nationalism encoded a powerful sense of 'African-ness', (of being African, although they had a Western culture). Hence, the invention of 'Afrikanerness' encoded a narrative beginning with 17th century rebellions against Dutch rule (so as to define a 'break with Europe').

Ultimately, the group of radical intellectuals who lay at the heart of Afrikaner Nationalism succeeded in interpellating a previously disparate group of people (divided by regionalism, class, and historical conflicts) into a new imaginary lived relationship called 'Afrikaner-ness'. A strong sense of 'own-ness' (around the notion of '*die volk*' [the people]) was created and naturalized. This was linked to an 'us-them' dichotomy in which the 'them' (Anglos, blacks and communists) were defined as threatening to *die volk*. Encoded into *die volk* was a strong sense of uniqueness; a group self-defined by its narrative as different from all around them because they were:

- Africans with European roots;
- Speaking a language spoken no-where else;
- Culturally Western-European and Christian (rather than African animists); and
- Racially distinct.

The narrative that was naturalized further defined this group as having a God-given right for self-defence/preservation (traceable back to the Battle of Blood River mythology of a 'pact with God'). On coming to power in 1948, the NP actioned these discourses in the following ways:

1. They banned the Communist Party.
2. White supremacy (adopted from the Milner model) and the ethnic/class-ranking model of racial capitalism were taken for granted, but were pushed further by taking the vote away from Cape coloureds.
3. They moved to halt Anglicization, while promoting the use of Afrikaans, and creating cultural spaces for 'own-ness'. In particular, the NP institutionalized ethnic-education, primarily to establish an Afrikaner cultural-space (i.e. schools, colleges, universities). Simultaneously, separate education departments were established for coloureds, Indians, urban blacks and for each black homeland.
4. The NP moved quickly to demolish the shack-land slums (e.g. Langlaagte, Lady Selbourne, Sophiatown, Cato Manor, and District Six), and resettle people into new, racially-defined, suburbs. From this was born South Africa's race-based urban planning model.

5. A de facto affirmative action program for Afrikaners was operated during the 1950s and 1960s, although it was never called this. The objective was to re-rank Afrikaners upwards within the Milner model and to upgrade the Afrikaner lumpenproletariat. To achieve this, the NP provided jobs (for example on the railways), and began building an extensive education infrastructure of Afrikaans-language schools, technical colleges, teachers' training colleges and universities. This was paid for by taxing South African capitalists, who tended to be Anglos. As a sweetener to these capitalists, the apartheid state facilitated the enhanced exploitation of black labour in order to facilitate higher profits. This affirmative action program was so successful that it eventually changed the NP's constituency. Hence, by the 1980/90s, the dramatically expanded Afrikaner middle classes no longer needed affirmative action or apartheid to 'upgrade' or protect them and had lost their hostility towards Anglos.
6. For intellectuals like Verwoerd, apartheid was also a response to the Atlantic Charter that threatened to bring majoritarian liberal-democracy to South Africa. This impending threat saw apartheid re-conceptualized as a form of internal de-colonization in the sense that each 'black nation' in South Africa would be given its own independent state as a means to ensure that one part of South Africa remained as a territorial-base for the Afrikaner nation. 'Own-ness' was to be territorialized and institutionalized as a series of nation-building projects. This necessarily involved abandoning the Milner white supremacy model (where whites would rule over blacks indefinitely), and replacing it with the idea that South Africa consisted of 11 separate nations. Ten of these 'nations' were black and they were to be granted self-rule and then independence (i.e. blacks

would no longer be ruled by whites). This shift was to produce an ever-expanding 'industry' of apartheid bureaucrats to set-up and administer the 'homeland policy'; an 'industry' that eventually became an important player in actually formulating policy.

7. A system of 'influx control' (using internal passports) was created to control black migration to the cities. The 'grand apartheid' vision was to actually reverse black migration through push-pull policies geared to shifting blacks out of the so-called 'white cities' and into the black homelands. A migrant labour system was institutionalized to allow contracted black workers into 'white' South Africa for limited periods of time. Under this policy, homeland blacks were deemed 'foreigners' in ('white') South Africa; with the NP arguing they were equivalent to Turkish 'guest-workers' in Germany. Supporters of apartheid used this logic to make apartheid more palatable to themselves; that is it was a means to avoid confronting the pain such policies caused in other people's lives.

In the process of implementing apartheid, the NP created a *verzuil*-ed South Africa - a country divided into ethnic compartments. The modernization, industrialization and process of racial-capitalist accumulation, initiated by Milner, continued apace under the NP, but it was not an Anglo or liberal-democratic modernization process. Instead, it was a modernization-program based upon high levels of state interventionism, and state planning based upon nationalist-socialist principles. This program specifically sought, using state funding, to intervene to promote the 'own-ness' of 13 language/cultural groups against the pressures of Anglo-modernization (as a way to justify protecting an Afrikaner national 'space').

The central failing of this model was its failure to accommodate South African (urban-based) Westernized blacks, especially those who had been substantively Anglicized in the highly industrialized Gauteng Province. Under apartheid these people were defined as citizens of the black homelands, and were expected to return to these homelands (thereby ceasing to be South Africans). Anti-apartheid resistance, centered upon the ANC, emerged from the failure to accommodate this black middle class. This produced ANC leaders like Mandela, Sisulu, Mbeki and Tambo. The apartheid state's response to the demands by Westernized blacks for political rights was militarization and repression. Ironically, this militarization generated further industrialization, which actually increased the flow of black people into South Africa's cities and so built a huge working class constituency for the ANC to mobilize.

Black Nationalism and Black Empowerment

Contemporary South African black nationalism is a by-product of racial-capitalism and its ethnic-ranking system. Just as Afrikaner nationalism was a form of 'catch-up nationalism' geared to re-arranging the order of the Anglo-colonial ranking system, so too is the black nationalism espoused by the ANC. The ANC's policies of 'black empowerment', 'corrective action' and 'affirmative action' are derivative of the fact that ethnicity and race have always served as powerful makers of status, life chances and identity in South Africa. In both British and apartheid South Africa, an ethnic ranking system placed whites at the top, Indians and coloureds in the middle and blacks at the bottom. A core feature of ANC policy has been state-intervention to undo the former 'racial hierarchy' and actively elevate the 'African majority' upwards (Jordan 1997:3) through black empowerment initiatives (Mbeki 1999: 2-3).

Contemporary South African black nationalism bears many resemblances to Afrikaner nationalism. Both share a similar set of contextual roots:

- The dislocation of urbanization and modernization triggered by the introduction of modernizing capitalism. Afrikaners underwent this dislocating process of urbanization following the Boer War, whereas black South Africans experienced these dislocations following World War II.
- The deprivations of poverty caused by being rural migrants into an urban environment for which one does not have the skills. Just as Afrikaners were poverty-stricken shack-land dwellers in the first half of the 20th century, so too were black South Africans in the second half. Where Afrikaners perceived Anglo-capitalists and British imperialism as their tormentors, black South Africans came to see capitalism and Afrikaner nationalists as their tormentors.
- The experience of being ranked badly within the (Empire-derived) ethnic-ranking structure created the same sense of resentment amongst first Afrikaners, and later blacks. Both were made to feel like foreigners and/or second-class citizens in their own country.

This experiential bundle of dislocation, deprivation and second-classedess was to generate both Afrikaner and black nationalism. This 'pain' can be clearly perceived in President Thabo Mbeki's (2000: 8) lament that South Africa remains "a country of two nations". Mbeki (2000: 2) referred to whites as the 'oppressor nation', 'colonialists' and "the arrogant …[who] … believe themselves to be superior". He reproached whites as "the beneficiaries of racism [who] consider it their duty to discourage the victims of racism from reflecting and acting on the pain they feel" (Mbeki 2000: 8). He noted that, unlike other colonial situations, in

South Africa "our own 'oppressor nation' and 'ruling class' ceased to be foreign" (Mbeki 2000: 3); remaining within the country. This created the challenge for black people to destroy the old order while having to continue to live within the same state as the 'oppressor nation'. Mbeki's first public airing of the notion that South Africa is a country of two nations was made in 1998 when Mbeki proposed that the notion of reconciliation needed to be reappraised because South Africa was not becoming one nation and would not become one nation, until substantive progress was made in upgrading the black peoples' socio-economic position (Mbeki 1998).

Not surprisingly, given that their contextual roots are so similar, both Afrikaner and South African black nationalists have developed similar policies to try to rectify the situations that they found intolerable. As Jesudason (1995: 7) has noted, they have sought to capture the state and then to use it to "modify the opportunity structure of society". In South Africa, black empowerment, corrective action and affirmative action represent the policies adopted by black people who have used the ANC to successfully take control of the state. Black South Africans, previously ranked 'backwards' (Horowitz 1985: 174) under racial capitalism (in both its Milnerite and apartheid forms), now demand that they be granted preferential treatment relative to those formally deemed to belong to the 'advanced' group. The objective is to ensure that those previously ranked 'backwards' now take charge politically so as to facilitate state-led upward-ranking initiatives (Jordan 1997: 3). Hence, from the 1990s onwards, South African black people (referring to themselves as 'the majority' or 'the previously disadvantaged') have demanded preferential employment opportunities, university placements etcetera, while whites (pejoratively referred to as 'the elite' or 'the minority') have been penalized. Businesses whose ownership and staffing structures were seen to be 'too white' were not given government contracts, and have been legislatively forced to meet race quotas. The ANC-government has also re-staffed the civil service and state-owned enterprises (by retrenching whites and replacing them with blacks).

The apartheid state built a military-industrial complex as part of its attempts to defend itself. This undermined a core feature of apartheid, namely 'influx control' because as the military-industrial complex expanded, the urbanization and modernization of black people increased. The apartheid state also needed ever-growing numbers of black people to staff its bureaucratic and security apparatus. Hence, the apartheid state expanded the urban black middle class and built an enormous black working class. These people experienced not only the dislocation of rapid urbanization, but also the trauma of having to function in an urban environment where they were treated as second-class within apartheid's ethnic-ranking structure. This produced the conditions for the growth of a highly aspirational black petit bourgeoisie, highly motivated to ethnically re-ranking South Africa. To achieve this, they needed to build precisely the 'imagined community' apartheid was trying to stop emerging, namely a unified 'black South Africa'. This involved interpellating disparate and divided groups of people into a new set of imaginary lived relationships. During the 1980s this was achieved by mobilizing a creative mix of black nationalist and socialist discourses. In the 1990s the socialist discourses were dropped in favour of an unbridled black nationalism geared to building a 'patriotic black bourgeoisie' (Malala 1996).

Those driving the policy of black empowerment are the black petit bourgeoisie who have the most to gain from its implementation. The largest concentration of South Africa's black petit bourgeoisie is found in the Gauteng Province (the Johannesburg, Witwatersrand, Pretoria, and

Vereeniging area). Gauteng's black community had its roots in every ethnic and tribal group in Southern Africa; it was a community born of an enormous urban cultural melting pot. The result was the growth of a new cultural form, particularly in Johannesburg, from the 1950s onwards, which could be termed 'Gauteng culture'. The Gauteng petit bourgeoisie are Westernized Africans who are increasingly bringing up their children with English as their first language. They constitute the new elite of compradors who have stepped into the shoes of the whites they have displaced in the government and business sectors. In this respect there are some strong resemblances to the so-called 'Wabenzi' elite in East Africa.

Ultimately, the new black comprador elite is the outcome of a liberal-reform agenda driven by the Urban Foundation (and funded by South African capitalists) from the 1970s onwards. This reformist program sought to build a strong black middle class in order to stabilize South African capitalism. During the anti-apartheid struggle this emergent black petit bourgeoisie aligned themselves with the black working class (institutionalized within the ANC-Communist Party-Congress of South African Trade Unions alliance). This alliance deployed socialist discourse (with many features of cut and paste Marxism) to mobilize the black working class that grew rapidly during the 1970/80s as the apartheid state built its industrial-military complex. After the collapse of the Soviet Union, this ANC-led alliance pragmatically modified its discourse. Whereas in the 1980s ethnic re-ranking was couched in terms of a socialist re-distribution of wealth, from the early 1990s it was re-couched in terms of 'affirmative action', borrowed from the United States' equal employment opportunities (EEO) discourse (Holloway 1989: 10), hence making it much more palatable to Washington. Overall, the way in which the ANC has shifted its worldview and narratives over time is highly instructive of how South Africa's black middle class intelligentsia has pragmatically adjusted its discourses to fit changing political circumstances. For example,

1. In the 1950s an Atlantic Charter discourse was used (for example, in the ANC's Freedom Charter). Deploying the discourse of 'majoritarianism', borrowed from US Atlantic Charter thinking, this served as a powerful rhetorical weapon to fight the NP while evoking Western sympathy.
2. From the 1960s to 1980s, Soviet patronage, and efforts to build working class support for the ANC, saw the adoption of a 'socialist redistribution' discourse.
3. The collapse of the Soviet Union brought a shift during the early 1990s to US-liberal discourses like 'affirmative action' and (capitalist) 'economic growth'. This shift has created some tensions within the ANC-led alliance.
4. During the interregnum period (when Afrikaners still dominated the civil service and security apparatus), the ANC replaced 'affirmative action' with 'corrective action'; a terminology that resonated with Afrikaner nationalist understandings of their own struggle against Anglo-domination.
5. Once the ANC felt securely in power, 'corrective action' was replaced with the more powerful nationalist term of 'black empowerment'.

Each of the above five processes effectively describes ethnic re-ranking of the sort described by Jesudason (1995).

One of the consequences of South Africa's 1990s affirmative action/corrective action programs was the rapid enlargement of South Africa's black middle class; a group that now effectively controls the ANC and/or the ruling (Mbeki) faction of the government. This black middle class has effectively been co-opted into a corporatist alliance with

South African capital, such that capitalism has been stabilized in accordance with the original Urban Foundation plans. In fact, this comprador elite has moved into those suburbs previously associated with the Anglo-business sector, and adopted the same lifestyle as those Anglos. The resultant assimilation into South African Anglo culture has served as a powerful mechanism to 'tame' many former radical ANC activists into so-called 'Gucci comrades'.

But this black middle class now finds itself occupying a set of contradictory positions. Foremost of these is a growing gap between this comprador elite and South Africa's black underclass who still effectively live at the bottom of the socio-economic system originally introduced by Milner's kindergarten. For the black middle class beneficiaries of affirmative action/black empowerment this creates tensions. On the one hand, they still mobilize a discourse of ethnic re-ranking that claims to be uplifting the entire 'black nation'. However, the majority of the black masses cannot be upgraded because the corporatist deal with South African capital precludes this possibility, as do the rules of globalization imposed by Pax Americana. The result has been the promotion of black nationalist discourses (e.g. 'African renaissance') by the new ruling group, who ANC politician Jabu Moleketi has described as a 'patriotic black bourgeoisie' (Malala 1996). This shift to black nationalism has generated for the 'patriotic bourgeoisie' one seemingly irresolvable 'identity' contradiction/tension associated with advocating 'Afrocentric' values and practices on the one hand, while on the other being centrally involved in administering a de facto Westernization process.

So what are the key discourses being deployed by South Africa's contemporary ruling elite? The following characterize their worldview:

1. Gautengers demographically dominate this middle class. Because this Gauteng middle class is the product of a modernization process that occurred under apartheid (Louw 1998: 151-152), this is a modern group of people unsympathetic to traditional African (pre-modern) values that remain associated with apartheid. The Gauteng middle class staunchly advocates enhanced modernization, and so have become the contemporary heirs of Milner's South African modernization project.
2. Under apartheid this urban group were designated as 'foreign' guest labourers. Being made to feel like underdogs and foreigners in their own country has generated pain and grievances that have translated into Jesudason's ethnic re-ranking response, seen most clearly in the policy of black empowerment.
3. Because apartheid promoted 'own-ness', this group is opposed to any hint of *verzuiling*-logic. Their discourses and policies effectively promote assimilation into Gauteng culture as well as the de facto Anglicization of South Africa.
4. Although this group widely deployed a socialist discourse during the anti-apartheid struggle, they have (in the process of pragmatically accommodating themselves to both the Pax Americana and a corporatist alliance with South African capital) become compradors for global-capitalism. The discomfort that many feel about this has translated itself in anti-Eurocentric-speak and/or an advocacy of Afrocentricism (which in South Africa means 'Gauteng culture'). This nationalist rhetoric appears to serve as a self-denial safety valve to release tension in the face of having been de facto co-opted and tamed by South African capital.
5. The ANC is now dominated by a 'patriotic black bourgeoisie' who are using their control of government to enrich themselves, while at the same time failing to de-

liver the promised post-apartheid nirvana to the country's huge black underclass. To remain in power, this black bourgeoisie needs to invent and popularize narratives that convince the black working class, lumpenproletariat and rural poor to follow them. To do this, they have invented the 'subject position' of 'blackness' as black nationalism has come to underpin their new project of 'nation building'. Essentially a single 'black nation' has been invented that fudges over the divisions of class, the cleavages between Western-urbanites and rural pre-moderns, linguistic and tribal divisions and the divisions between blacks who fought for and against apartheid. The 'patriotic black bourgeoisie' has effectively deployed a set of discourses that invites all 'blacks' to become part of an 'us' within an us-them dichotomy. This dichotomy under-writes 'black empowerment' which in turn further enriches the black middle classes.

CONCLUSION

After coming to power in 1994, the ANC's central policy-agenda became affirmative action (which subsequently mutated into corrective action and then black empowerment). Out of this has emerged an ever-expanding black middle class tied to a patronage-system that relies on the state to enforce the transfer of resources and opportunities into black hands. In some respects the ANC's black empowerment program appears to simply replicate the NP's ethnic patronage system. However, there are some significant differences from the NP's model because the ANC program is not based upon building a separate and parallel set of infrastructures. Instead, it is based upon taking control of *existent* socio-economic structures in order to promote black (middle class) interests. Significantly, the NP's affirmative action program (because it was based on 'own-ness') created *separate* parallel Afrikaner structures, where initially 'standards' were not as high (i.e. Afrikaners were effectively 'protected' from Anglo competition while standards were raised over a 20 year period). This meant the business sector was not 'damaged' by having less competent people forced on them by Afrikaner affirmative action. Aside from increased taxation and having to comply with 'influx control' regulations, the Anglo business sector was left largely unscathed by Afrikaner nationalism during the affirmative action up-grade/transition period. Afrikaner nationalism succeeded in modifying societies' opportunity structures in ways that did not damage the Anglo-dominated economy created by Milner. This left the state's tax-base unscathed, and did not generate a major exodus of skilled and entrepreneurial Anglos. The same is not true of the ANC's current black empowerment policies, which are far more interventionist because they seek direct and immediate access to *existent* socio-economic infrastructures. However, despite the disruptions this nationalist interventionism is causing, South African capital continues to treat the patriotic black bourgeoisie as a valuable post-apartheid corporatist-alliance partner; because the ANC (dominated by this patriotic bourgeois faction) serves to stabilize capitalism by managing the huge black underclass. Essentially, the basic outlines of Milner's modern capitalist state can only be preserved if this black middle class can successfully continue to 'buy off' the black underclass through 'symbolic-delivery' (i.e. black nationalist narratives instead of economic-delivery). In return for managing the underclasses, the parasitic nature of the patriotic black bourgeoisie (and even its tendencies towards crony-capitalism), will be tolerated as preferable to the alternative of having to seriously re-design the socio-economic and state infrastructures (originally codified by the 'Kindergarten').

So, for the moment, South Africa's future looks strangely like its past. The basic outlines of the Milner model having remained intact, while nationalism and ethnic re-ranking continue as the dominant discourses (albeit that 'black' rather than 'Afrikaner' nationalism is now dominant). Understanding the continuities and similarities between apartheid and post-apartheid South Africa is made possible by getting 'into the heads' of Afrikaner and black nationalists and examining how their discourses and narratives are ultimately rooted in similar experiences of the modernizing racial-capitalist state, the elements of which Milner and his kindergarten originally drew together and codified a century ago.

REFERENCES

Althusser, L. (1971) *Lenin, Philosophy & Other Essays,* London: New Left Books.

Anderson, B. (1991) *Imagined Communities. Reflections on the Origin and Spread of Nationalism,* London: Verso.

Boulding, K. (1956) *The Image,* Ann Arbour, Michigan: University of Michigan Press.

De Klerk, W.A. (1975) *The Puritans in Africa,* Harmondsworth: Pelican Books.

George, A. (1969) 'The 'Operational Code': a Neglected Approach to the Study of Political Leaders and Decision-Making', *International Studies Quarterly*, 13, pp. 190-222.

Hall, S. (1977) 'Culture, the Media and the 'Ideological Effect' in J. Curran, M. Gurevitch & J. Woollacott (eds), *Mass Communication and Society,* London: Edward Arnold.

Headlam, C. (1933) *The Milner Papers, Vol 11,* London: Cassell & Co Ltd.

Heck, M.C. (1980) 'The Ideological Dimension of Media Messages', in S. Hall, D.

Hobson, A. Lowe, & P. Willis (eds), *Culture, Media, Language,* London: Hutchinson.

Herd, N. (1966) *1922: The Revolt on the Rand,* Johannesburg: Blue Crane Books.

Holloway, F.A. (1989) 'What is Affirmative Action?', in F. Blanchard & F. Crosby (eds), *Affirmative Action in Perspective,* New York: Springer-Verlag.

Horowitz, D. (1985) *Ethnic Groups in Conflict,* Berkeley: University of California Press.

Jesudason, J. (1995) 'The Ethnic Factor in Development,' in J. Ravenhill, (ed), *Singapore, Indonesia, Malaysia, The Philippines and Thailand. Vol II,* Aldershot (UK): Elgar Reference Collection.

Jordan, P. (1997) *The National Question in Post 1994 South Africa,* Discussion paper for the ANC's 50th National Conference, Mafikeng (December).

Kitching G. (2000) 'Why I Gave Up African Studies', *African Studies Review and Newsletter*, 22 (1), pp.21-26.

Louw P. & Tomaselli, K. (1991) 'Semiotics of Apartheid: The Struggle for the Sign', *European Journal for Semiotic Studies*, 3(1), pp. 99-110.

Louw, P.E. (1998) 'Diversity Versus National Unity: The Struggle Between Moderns, Premoderns and Postmoderns in Contemporary South Africa', in D. Tanno, & A. Gonzales (eds), *Communication and Identity Across Cultures*, London: Sage.

Malala, Justice (1996), 'Government Aims to Build a New Bourgeoisie', *The Star*, (22 May).

Mbeki, T. (1999) Speech at the Annual National Conference of the Black Management Forum, Kempton Park, 20 November.

Mbeki, T. (2000) 'Where are they now?' Second National Institute for Economic Policy Oliver Tambo Lecture, Johannesburg (11 August).

Nimocks, W. (1968) *Milner's Young Men: the 'Kindergarten in Edwardian Imperial Affairs',* Durham: Duke University Press.

O'Meara, D. (1983) *Volkskapitalism. Class, Capital and Ideology in the Development of Afrikaner Nationalism,* Johannesburg: Ravan.

Rokeach, M. (1960) *The Open and Closed Mind,* New York: Basic Books.
Steyn, J. (1987) *Trouwe Afrikaners,* Cape Town: Tafelberg.
Volosinov, V.N. (1973) *Marxism and the Philosophy of Language,* New York: Seminar Press.

Chapter 4

Two Worlds: Integration, Synthesis or Conflict? Psychological Perspectives on Cultural Identity in Africa

Jane Gilbert

Being between the ‘two worlds’ of African and Western values and cultural belief systems can sometimes have profound psychological effects on a person’s sense of belonging and rootedness. Internal uncertainty or conflict in relation to individual identity can result in anxiety, reduced self confidence, denial of childhood experience and cultural roots, and secret adherence to beliefs and rituals. It is the theme of this paper that such personal experience of cultural conflict directly mirrors conflicts in cultural identity within emerging African nations, and that an understanding of one can aid an understanding of the other.

Personal Identity

Personal identity can be defined as an individual’s own sense of who s/he is. It has two sources: an individual’s unique history, experiences and perceptions; and membership of, and affiliation with, various social groups, including national groups. Thus, a person's sense of self/identity is simultaneously both individual and social (Searle-White 2001). Therefore, it always encompasses a number of different 'selves', including, inter alia, those based on family, territory, class, religion, occupation, ethnicity and gender. Everyone experiences parts of their personal identity differently depending upon the social context; for example, a woman will experience one part of her identity when she is being a mother with her children, and another, probably quite different part when she is in a work context. A particular 'self' can be evoked and become more salient in some situations and not others, while particular social circumstances also reinforce certain parts of personal identity more than others. Because inside each person there are many different selves/identities, there will be occasions when some of these internal 'selves' may be experienced as being in conflict with each other.

National Identity

The concept of a nation/nationality as the primary means of defining collective identity is a Western, relatively modern view. This Western model of national identity can be defined as "a named population sharing a historical territory, common myths and historical memories, a mass public culture, a common economy and common legal rights and duties for all its members" (Smith 1991:14). The process of colonisation, in which Western countries defined and divided territory in Africa into 'nations' with limited regard for tribal affiliations, has resulted in the Western notion of national identity being the primary influence on how African nations have formulated the development of their own national identities after independence.

This Western, historically recent, concept of national identity is fundamentally different from the understanding of national identity in non-Western cultures. In this very different cultural viewpoint, a nation is regarded predominantly as a community of common descent, in which *common ancestry* and genealogy are of paramount importance, rather than boundaries or a common economy. The establishment of national identities in emerging African nations after independence is also made more difficult because tribal identities, based on specific belief systems, historical narratives and indigenous languages unique to a tribal group, have been subject to consistent erosion. This erosion has been exacerbated by the imposition of other cultural belief systems and languages by Christian missionaries and, more recently, the onslaught of cultural globalisation. The secure personal and national identities of the past, expressed in specific tribal and language groups, have been threatened, and, in many contexts, lost. Within all African nations this loss has been exacerbated by the development of an education system based on Western cultural assumptions, and the development of an elite whose cultural background is predominantly Western. Members of this elite may no longer teach their children the cultural understandings or language of their tribe, and thus, each generation is further removed from parts of their own traditional cultural identity.

Threats to Personal and National Identity

Personal identity, and the different 'selves' of which it is composed, cannot exist without social context and validation by others. Identity is thus sometimes experienced as fragile and potentially at risk, and can be threatened and changed in very different ways. For example, new problems or challenges in someone's personal circumstances may initiate changes in personal identity, i.e. becoming a parent for the first time. Change may also occur through gradual influence and interactions with others, for example if someone goes to live in another country. Change can also be imposed on both individuals and societies by deliberate social re-engineering and control, for example the passing of laws forbidding behaviour or customs previously considered socially acceptable. A number of significant changes in African countries have been of the latter kind; imposed by colonialism, by missionaries, by Western technology and now by the process of cultural globalisation.

Examples of the imposition of cultural change can be seen in relation to many African government institutions. According to Smith (1991: 106), the administrative apparatus of the colonial state was a 'hybrid', "an alien executive instrument from a culturally different political community". Even today, most independent African countries still have formal institutions that were transplanted from a European cultural context by the colonists. These institutions were superimposed upon the existing indigenous, tribal based, authority structures and informal historical networks. In many instances this has resulted in a profound disconnection between formal institutions, which have their roots in European cultural traditions, and the informal traditional networks that still powerfully affect people's lives and their sense of cultural identity.

All cultures evolve and change over time, but it is of extreme significance that recent and present immense cultural upheavals are not taking place gradually and organically as in earlier periods of history. Colonisation of other cultures has taken place throughout history, but advanced communications technology now enables the images and cultural value systems from the dominant American/European global cultures to be transmitted into every country in the world. Power and influence can now be exercised on a worldwide scale. Thus, threats to cultural identities are now greater than at any time in history.

LOSS AND CHANGE

Irreversible social and cultural changes in individual and cultural identity can result in acute experiences of emotional loss. According to Marris (1996), experiences of loss fundamentally disrupt the ability to find meaning, and can be evoked by any situation where the ability to make sense of life is severely disrupted. The resulting psychological processes are therefore extremely similar to the processes experienced in reaction to the loss experienced in personal bereavement.

Attachment is essential to a sense of emotional security for all human beings, and any loss that robs someone of an attachment profoundly disrupts their ability to experience life in the same meaningful way as before. This occurs no matter how 'rational' or 'beneficial' changes may seem to another person who does not have the same intensity of attachment. The process of grieving in reaction to the loss of something to which a person has been intensely attached can be seen in all cultures (Murray Parkes 1998), and can be a reaction to change in any area of someone's life, not only in response to death. The severity of grief is directly dependent upon the person's *intensity* of emotional attachment to what has been lost, not the actual object of attachment. For example, people can experience grief regarding the loss of their old home, even when, in a material sense, the new house may be thought of by others as an 'improvement'. People can experience grief from the loss of religious rituals that they have carried out since their own childhood and to which they are intensely emotionally attached, although to others without such attachments, they may have little meaning. Some parents experience grief at the end of their own children's childhood, as the meaning of their own lives has to be renegotiated. Grief can also be experienced at the loss of employment by which someone defined their identity. This painful loss of meaning can also occur in circumstances where someone's language, customs or ways of living are altered by social and cultural change. Adaptation to new circumstances, where something to which a person has been emotionally attached has been lost, requires psychological reintegration. Previous meanings by which a person has made sense of a part of his/her life are no longer valid, and new meanings to make sense of new life situations have to be reconstituted.

Reactions to Loss

If change is understood as a process of loss of meaning requiring psychological integration, what reactions can be expected? Normal processes of grief contain intense anxiety and despair. If the predictability of events has been invalidated by loss, continuity of meaning has to be restored before life will feel manageable again. A person who has suffered loss engages in active psychological searching for *threads of continuity* in their experience which will help to restore a sense that what has been lost can still give meaning to the present. Somehow, the purpose and feeling that the particular attachment expressed has to be abstracted from its past setting and reformulated so as to make sense in the present and the future. Feelings of grief cannot be assuaged by a substitute because meaning has been inextricably bound up with the *specific* attachment that has been lost.

In seeking to predict how people will cope with loss, in relation to both personal and socio-cultural identity, some of the essential questions to be considered are as follows: do the changes 'make sense' to the person? can meaning be attributed to the changes in light of the cultural meanings and attachments within which the person has grown up? and can any purpose be derived from the changes? If one asks these questions in the context of cultural change in Africa, some of the ambiguities, contradictions and conflicts that engender feelings of loss become apparent, and, in addition, some of the inherent contradictions within Western culture are also illuminated. What follows are only very brief examples of some fundamental questions.

What effects does the promotion of Western cultural and economic value systems including materialism, wasteful consumption and ecological damage have on those who have been brought up with cultural values that are very different? What effects might the promotion of these very different cultural values have on an individual's experience of his own cultural identity? Does s/he feel a sense of belonging or alienation? How is a villager to make sense of the gross inequalities in nutrition, life expectancy, education, and material standard of living between what is portrayed in media images of Western countries and his/her own experience? How does someone make sense of the meaning of his/her own life? Does the exposure to the two worlds make someone feel more certain and attached to their own culture or do they experience anxiety and anger? How does someone feel when the language in which their deepest feelings are expressed is considered irrelevant, and the customs by which the person's own community has made sense of life and experience are implicitly devalued by the 'development' in his own country? Marris (1996: 67-8) describes some aspects of the experience as follows:

> What do wealth, status, marriage, honour mean for an African villager in a society where traditional, colonial and autonomous national institutions overlay each other in such rapid succession that the values and symbols of three different periods in history, each derived from a different framework of assumptions, are present all at once? The loss of meaning is not as abrupt and overwhelming as in bereavement, but it is

> *cumulative* [my emphasis], as the implications of the creation of nation states work themselves out . . . In these circumstances he is caught between the same conflicting impulses as the bereaved – to return to the past, which seems in retrospect a haven of security and meaningful satisfactions; to realise at once a new self, a modern man confidently handling the possibilities of a progressive nation. Each impulse provokes its painful reaction; the attempt to revive tradition only exposes its decay; the pursuit of modernity leads to humiliating frustrations and bewilderment, and a sense of betrayal of his true identity.

Attempts to superimpose a different set of cultural assumptions on traditional ways of being and thinking ignore the reality of earlier fundamental structures of meaning, the conventions used to express them, and the processes of loss involved in such changes. *Enforced* and extremely rapid changes in cultural identity, both national and personal, are likely to produce acute experiences of loss and bereavement, particularly in relation to cultural and language frameworks. Although the processes of change and loss are continuous within every culture, and every generation has specific losses and changes to which it must adapt, the recent processes of cultural change in Africa have been far more rapid, of a greater magnitude and much more profound than in earlier historical time frames or in other cultures. It is therefore not surprising that enforced social change at many different levels has brought disorder, disorientation, anger and resentment.

NATION OR TRIBE? THE TOLERANCE OF AMBIVALENCE

As mentioned above, the resulting process of grief from the loss of perceived earlier cultural identities, is very similar to bereavement, and contains a conflict between two contradictory impulses; to return to the past to recover the part of one's (the society's) identity that has been lost, or to behave as if it had not even existed. Returning to the past denies the reality of the changes in the present, but conversely, denying the past betrays the past experiences and meanings on which personal and national identity has been built. These conflicting impulses are experienced both nationally and personally, and to find ways forward for the future the conflict and ambivalence has to somehow be reconciled.

The question of tribalism in African nations illustrates this ambivalence. When an individual defines him/herself by tribe, superficially this would seem to be inconsistent with the desire to establish a single nation. However, the problems that arise from tribalism in African nations represent the crucial questions; the conflicting impulses which must be reconciled. The larger social processes of establishing cultural identity are reflected in individual experience; each is a reflection of the other. Both individual and national responses to the passing of traditional society and cultural change are often ambivalent.

A recent workshop for university staff in Ghana facilitated by the author revealed clearly that, even though all the participants had completed Western style education to post-graduate level, most still defined their *primary* personal identity by tribe, and the majority preferred to speak their mother tongue. At the same time, all also accepted and believed in the need for Ghana to be a single nation with English as the common language. Participants were also very explicit in their feelings of loss regarding traditional aspects of their own culture. Discussions illuminated this state of ambivalence; nostalgia and deep attachment to their own tribal and traditional cultural identities, but simultaneously a commitment to the ideal of a single nation.

Defining identity by tribe can be seen as an expression of the need to maintain the threads of cultural continuity from the past and to find a relevant strategy for dealing with modern life. Attachment to tribe is both a challenge to emerging nations and a search for meaning in individual identity in the face of losses from the past and confusion regarding identity in the present and future. The conflict between establishing a single national identity and maintaining allegiance to tribe can thus be understood as a means of protecting both individuals and nations against what can seem unbearable contradictions. It is also an essential part of the ambivalent process necessary in loss and mourning whereby threads of continuity in meaning between past, present and future have to be established.

If the search for reconciliation and threads of continuity between past and future is abandoned, the political risks are likely to be one of two extremes: division and conflict on tribal lines or uncompromising nationalism which ignores tribal loyalties. Both are problematic. The struggle for cultural identity, in both individuals and nations, can only be worked out through a long process of reinterpretation, by which essential understandings of life are abstracted from traditional contexts and reformulated (Marris 1996: 67-8). Because these processes in reaction to loss are essential, any attempts to pre-empt conflict or ambivalence by rational planning, or by the imposition of political systems, will be unsuccessful. Demands by Western institutions for African nations to develop their cultural identities in ways that are similar to the dominant Western global culture can be profoundly disrespectful. Such demands do not sufficiently take into account different cultural meanings, value systems and language, and also deny the processes of loss which automatically occur with the imposition of Western global culture.

Cultural Identity and 'Development'

How do individuals and emerging African nations forge cultural identities which encompass the ambivalent processes of loss and bereavement and incorporate sufficient threads of continuity from their own past to survive the onslaught of American/European global culture? Smith (1991: 73) states that "every nation has its particular 'genius', its own ways of acting, thinking, communicating, and [that] emerging African nations must work to discover that unique genius wherever it is lost". However, according to Mabawonku et al (2001), basing cultural identity on African ways of approaching life and specifically African cultural values is conceptually and practically difficult because of the institutional disconnections caused by the 'two worlds' discussed previously and the problems of hunger. Even though much of Africa has abundant natural resources, many government policies are now driven by the effects of hunger and poverty, making the cultural values of people and nations even more difficult to define.

The concept of 'development' in relation to the cultural identities of African nations, and by implication individuals, is a further confounding factor. As a concept it seems misleading and patronising. As Sachs (1992: 1) suggests, "[t]he idea of development stands like a ruin in the intellectual landscape ... Its shadow obscures our vision.". In spite of 'aid' and so-called 'development' projects, problems in Africa continue to worsen and the gap between rich and poor countries is actually greater than it was 50 years ago. It is questionable whether the concept of 'development', with its implicit assumptions of Western superiority and devaluation of other cultural belief systems, is actually useful for emerging African nations, and the expectation from international organisations that African countries must have a national identity and similar societal systems to Western countries show little recognition, acceptance or respect for different cultural understandings.

Western science and technology can benefit African countries in many ways, but in other respects the price paid is very high. In too many instances science and technology have not been adapted to fit specifically African contexts, and what is to be treasured in uniquely African traditional cultural values has not been sufficiently identified, articulated and retained with any clarity. The arrogance underlying Western scientific methodology that all problems can somehow be 'solved' by technological 'progress', has not only had deleterious and destructive social and environmental effects worldwide, but also explicitly devalues different cultural understandings such as the intuitive wisdom and knowledge within the oral traditions characteristic of African cultures.

Excess consumption by affluent countries is depleting the world's natural resources and contributing to environmental degradation, and the adverse effects of technology on human relationships are only now being fully recognised. Unfettered market forces and the power of global business corporations have been catastrophic for trade in much of Africa, and the ideology of materialism which translates all areas of life into commodities that can be bought and sold, is the major cause of depersonalisation and spiritual emptiness in the West (Moore 1997). In addressing the onslaught of American/European cultural globalisation in African nations, the questions then become: will there be integration, synthesis or conflict in the process of adaptation? can the mistakes of Western cultures, environmentally, socially and psychologically, be recognised and addressed with the necessary efforts made to avoid their replication in African countries? and can African countries maintain their own unique 'genius', their own ways of acting, thinking, communicating, without succumbing to the new colonialism of American/European cultural globalisation? Recovery from grief, at both personal and national levels, depends on restoring a sense that lost attachments can still give meaning to the present, not on finding new substitutes. The purpose and feelings that past attachments and meanings expressed have to be somehow abstracted from past settings and reformulated. This transition must incorporate the past and continue its ideals. Integrating elements and meanings from the past will enable continuity of meaning for the present and future.

INTEGRATION, SYNTHESIS OR CONFLICT?

At present there seems little hope that the ever-increasing dominance of American/European culture and values can be halted, so is an integration or synthesis with African cultural understandings possible? Integration might be thought most likely to achieve the best of the 'two worlds', but the following apparently 'simple' example by Mabowonku (2001) describing the integration of traditional medicine with orthodox medical practice in Primary Health Care in Nigeria is given to briefly illustrate some very profound difficulties.

At present 58% of Nigeria's population utilise traditional medicine, and, on the surface, it seems very reasonable to attempt to integrate this into the Primary Health Care system based on orthodox Western medicine. However, the integration of one with the other is inherently problematic on many levels. As an example of this emerging integration, Mabowonku (2001) describes the increasing use of Western based medical systems by traditional healers in Nigeria, including marketing, public relations, packaging and standardization of traditional herbal remedies; practices alien to traditional African culture. The fundamental incompatibility between the institutional frameworks of traditional medicine and those of Western systems of knowledge remains. The problem with attempting integration of the two in the example described by Mabowonku is that, because of the supposed 'superiority' of Western scientific methodology, there is enormous pressure for traditional knowledge and understandings to be 'packaged' to fit Western systems of knowledge. Thus, Western methodology is still paramount, and there is a great danger that the *scientific* model (a model totally at variance with other cultural understandings of disease and illness) underpinning Western medical practice will simply be replicated, while the essence of specifically African understandings, preserved orally through generations within very different knowledge frameworks, will be lost. Even the 'simple' translation of traditional approaches to medicine from indigenous languages into English also automatically results in the loss of complex cultural understandings. If integration of traditional and Western medical systems assumes the 'superiority' of Western methodology, there are real dangers that the experience of healing is itself then fundamentally changed. By attempting to fit traditional medicine into Western knowledge frameworks, rather than Western systems adapting to African cultural understandings, the unique and culturally specific African gifts of healing may be lost (Gilbert 1999).

PROPOSED CONTRIBUTIONS TO AFRICAN LEADERSHIP INITIATIVES

Continuing globalisation of American/European culture means that ongoing cultural change within Africa is inevitable and that the issues of integration, synthesis or conflict between the 'two worlds' will further affect all African people, both individually and nationally. Continuing cultural change requires leaders able to straddle enormous cultural divides and provide a clear vision of national identity for their peoples. The complex demands of leadership have been recognised in many African countries and specific leadership initiatives have been set up. It is suggested that the psychological perspectives discussed in this paper and their implications in practice could make a potentially valuable contribution to the curricula of such programmes.

In summary, it is suggested that the following fundamental principles in relation to loss and socio-cultural change have to be acknowledged and accepted:

- All human beings have a profound need to maintain consistency and to sustain familiar attachments and understandings which make life meaningful.
- Some socio-cultural changes, at both individual and societal levels, involve the irretrievable loss of important attachments Thus, processes of grief will occur.
- Too many changes in too short a time break down emotional resilience. In terms of the rapidity of social change and the onslaught of cultural globalisation upon African nations, it is imperative that the human need for continuity between past and present is recognised.
- It is essential to make clear what crucial purposes and attachments seem threatened by changes and then explore how these purposes can be retrieved and reformulated in different contexts in the future.
- What is familiar needs to be made to serve a purpose and attempts be made to rehabilitate familiar forms when possible before decisions are made as to what to destroy.
- The process of change must always expect and even encourage conflict. Whenever people are confronted with change they need the opportunity to react, to articulate their own ambivalent feelings and work out their own sense of it.

- Change requires time and patience because conflicts involve not just the accommodation of different interests, but also the establishment of an essential continuity in structures of meaning.
- In conflict it is essential to respect the autonomy of different kinds of experience, to accept that individuals and groups will react to change differently, and to recognise the need of every group to find its own sense of continuity.
- It must be acknowledged that all individuals love particular places, people, language, rituals, kinds of work, and cannot readily substitute for them by any generalised calculation of well being.
- If adaptation to change inhibits and does not explicitly acknowledge the need for these enduring attachments, a satisfying meaning to life will not be achieved and there will be nagging doubt about identity.
- If people are not able, and are not helped, to react in articulate ways to the threats of disintegration of their own culture and identity, their sense of loss will turn inward resulting in apathy, depression, cynicism, guilt and violence.
- If changes are disruptive and frequent, people lose confidence that their own lives have a meaningful continuity of purpose.
- If people cannot make sense of changes in terms of their own experience, they will become aimless or cynical even when changes may be intelligent and necessary.

These principles need to be placed within the context of an historical study of the contributions of the visionary leaders that Africa has produced in the past. Greater understanding of the qualities of African leaders of the past may help to identify what factors could be utilised in the present. In addition, incorporating psychological perspectives on loss and identity within African leadership initiatives could be facilitated in the following ways:

i) Individual Mentoring

The individual examination of a leader's own experiences of psychological cultural conflict. This would include, in particular, reflecting on the culture of their own childhood, subsequent education and experience in other cultures, and identifying their own internal strategies for dealing with internal psychological conflict. Participants would develop increased confidence through this personal knowledge, be able to articulate and share their understandings with others, and further develop their own strategies for integrating the diverse aspects of their cultural backgrounds.

ii) Participative Workshops

Workshops would review the processes involved in individual internal cross cultural psychological conflict, but apply this to societal perspectives on their own tribe and nation. The psychological effects of cultural globalisation could be considered in terms of different social groups within their own societies. Participants would consider how the process of cultural globalisation might be contained, develop greater clarity regarding the disadvantages of Western global culture, and articulate more clearly what is to be treasured in African traditions.

Conclusion

The larger socio-cultural processes of change are directly reflected in individual experience, and individuals and leaders must confront and negotiate cultural transformations within themselves which used to be experienced in generational change. It is imperative to search for new ways to interpret the past, provide a clear vision for the future, and enable processes of change to be respectful and humane. With the worldwide onslaught of American/European culture, threats to national and personal cultural identity have never been greater. Ever increasing numbers of people within Africa will experience the internal psychological conflict of the 'two worlds'. It seems essential that potential leaders in African countries examine such psychological perspectives, that facilitation is provided such that internal psychological processes can be examined and discussed openly, and that strategies for increased mental well-being are developed. Through understanding their own experiences of cultural conflict, and becoming more articulate in describing this process, potential leaders would have increased self knowledge, leading to greater self confidence. This personal understanding would also ensure a greater sensitivity to others, and leaders would be more adept and personally equipped to actively facilitate change within their own countries.

REFERENCES

Gilbert, J. (1999) 'Responding to Mental Distress: Cultural Imperialism or the Struggle for Synthesis?' *Development in Practice*, 9(3), pp. 287-295.

Mabawonku, A. (2001) 'Cultural Change in Traditional Medical Practice: the Search for an Appropriate Policy Response', Project proposal, Development Policy Centre, Agodi-Ibadan, Nigeria.

Mabawonku, A,. Jibiri, N. & Fasunwon, O. (2001) *Cultural Challenges for the Development of Science and Technology in Africa,* Paper presented at the International Symposium on Technology and Development in Africa, University of Illinois, Chicago, USA.

Marris, P. (1996) *Loss and Change,* London: Routledge.

Moore, T. (1997) *Care of the Soul,* London: Judy Piatkus (Publishers).

Murray Parkes, C. (1998) 'Understanding Grief Across Cultures', *Psychiatry in Practice,* 3, pp. 5-6.
Sachs, W. (1992) *The Development Dictionary,* London: Zed.
Searle-White, J. (2001) *The Psychology of Nationalism,* New York: Palgrave.
Smith, A.D. (1991) *National Identity,* London: Penguin Books.

Chapter 5

'The Second Betrayal?' Commemorating the 10th Anniversary of the Rwandan Genocide

Colin Cameron

As the 10th anniversary of the Rwandan genocide approaches, there are increasing moves to commemorate it internationally. Centring around an organization known as 'Remembering Rwanda', the aim is to ensure that memory of the genocide is preserved and "not be allowed to disappear" (Remembering Rwanda). There are a number of prominent individuals and groups now affiliated with 'Remembering Rwanda', including the former head of the United Nations Assistance Mission to Rwanda (UNAMIR), Romeo Dallaire, and Ingvar Carlsson, Chair of the Independent Inquiry into the role of the United Nations in Rwanda. In 1999, the Carlsson Inquiry confirmed officially that there had been a 'failure' to prevent the genocide. It is this sense of failure and subsequent betrayal of Rwanda that is motivating the organization. In keeping with the understanding that genocide represents the greatest example of human atrocity, various Holocaust memorial organizations have also offered support to the activities of 'Remembering Rwanda'. Daniel Libeskind, the architect who designed the Holocaust Museum in Berlin, has agreed to design a memorial for Rwandan genocide. Within Rwanda itself, 'Remembering Rwanda' has been endorsed by the rector of the National University of Rwanda, as well as *Ibuka* and *Avega* (organizations representing survivors of the genocide). The current Rwandan Government, installed by the Rwandan Patriotic Front (RPF) after they gained power in July 1994, has also endorsed 'Remembering Rwanda'.

Given the scale of what occurred in Rwanda during 1994, it is perhaps fitting that the 10th anniversary of the genocide be commemorated in such a way in April 2004. Although there have been annual commemoration ceremonies held in Rwanda since 1995, each anniversary of the genocide has failed to attract significant international attention. 'Remembering Rwanda' will then, be attempting to publicize as widely as possible the 10th anniversary. An increasing number of individuals and organizations have chosen to participate and organise commemoration ceremonies both locally and internationally. 'Remembering Rwanda' will be coordinating these ceremonies in order to preserve the memory of the genocide. The apparent urgency behind 'Remembering Rwanda' is the understanding that Rwanda itself will be now be betrayed once more if the genocide is not commemorated. For Gerald Kaplan (2003), the director of 'Remembering Rwanda,' the genocide is now "an event the world has totally forgotten"; a forgetting that amounts to a "second betrayal of Rwanda" (Kaplan 2003). The first 'betrayal' was seen as the failure to prevent the genocide and the subsequent abandonment of the Rwandan population; the second is the risk that it will be forgotten merely 10 years after it occurred. Consequently, any failure to commemorate the genocide internationally not only constitutes further 'betrayal', but will also allow the 'world' to remain indifferent to what occurred in Rwanda.

Also motivating 'Remembering Rwanda' is the belief that the 1994 genocide was unique. Although there have been other instances of genocide, what distinguishes the Rwandan genocide is both the manner in which it was realized and the assumption that it could have been prevented. Almost 10 years after it occurred, discussion of what happened in Rwanda is usually introduced with reference to the way in which the genocide was committed. The genocide is seen to be characterized by a certain 'intimacy', in that neighbours were called upon to kill neighbours. While this partially reflects what happened in Rwanda, privileging this intimacy as a putatively unique feature of the genocide reinforces the generalization that the genocide was committed simply by the Hutu majority against the minority Tutsi. Treating this as a unique characteristic not only obscures the extremely complex nature of social identity, for instance, the President of the *interahamwe*, Robert Kajuga, was himself Tutsi, but also ignores the fact that both Hutu and Tutsi were killed. Many Hutu were killed for either refusing to participate in the genocide, for sheltering Tutsi, or simply for material gain. Even for those who claim familiarity with Rwanda, the categories of Hutu and Tutsi are often posited as identifiable causes of the genocide. This has led to explanations centering on either the quiescent nature of the Rwandan population, the social discrimination against the Tutsi as a prerequisite for genocide, or that the explanation for the genocide lays in the mythological history of Hutu. Although there is little doubt that the deontological and mythical understanding of Hutu and Tutsi continues to have salience, perhaps more so now since 1994, seeing this as unique fails to account for what it was that actually precipitated the genocide; the war launched by the RPF from Uganda in 1990.

Emphasizing the 'intimacy' of the genocide rests also on the assumption that a significant proportion of the population participated, or that a significant number had to have participated in the genocide owing to the scale of what occurred. For 'Remembering Rwanda,' the nature of what happened in Rwanda has resulted in the unprecedented situation that survivors are required to live, invariably, amongst the perpetrators of the genocide. Despite the difficulties in trying to ascertain the composition of the Rwandan population since 1994, as well as the large scale villigisation (*imidugugu*) programs carried out by the Rwandan government (van Leeuwen 2001), the desire to commemorate the genocide internationally will, it is believed, also help with reconciliation between Hutu and Tutsi. For 'Remembering Rwanda', and the many other organizations involved in Rwanda, commemorating the genocide is not only necessary to remind the 'world' of its betrayal, it will serve to draw Hutu and Tutsi together. In this view, commemorating and maintaining the memory of what occurred is necessary to ensure that the divisive practices of the past that culminated in genocide are not repeated.

The genocide is also recurrently described as 'low tech' due to the use of common agricultural tools, requiring not only mass participation, but also extreme physical effort. Phillip Gourevitch (1995), whose work first appeared in *The New Yorker* and later published the most well known account of the genocide, consistently reiterates this. "By comparison", Gourevitch (1995: 78) writes, "Pol Pot's slaughter of a million Cambodians in four years looks amateurish, and the bloodletting in the former Yugoslavia measures up as little more than a neighbourhood riot". Privileging these supposedly unique features of the genocide in the way that Gourevitch's work has done, has resulted in an aesthetic understanding of what occurred in Rwanda genocide. Free from any consideration of what is still unknown about the genocide, such as who was responsible for assassinating President Habyarimana, whose death immediately preceded the genocide, the actual planning of the genocide, the killings by the RPF, or the way in which the genocide has become subject to ideological interpretation since 1994; it is this aesthetic understanding of Rwanda's uniqueness that now predominates.

The most searing example of this is the frequent reference to the rate of killing during the three months of the genocide. This particular aspect is seen as unique because despite the 'low tech' nature of the genocide, it was presumably more effective than the genocide conducted by the Nazis. Calculated as continuing for 'one hundred days,' the duration of the genocide itself has become emblematic, as the rate of killing between April and July 1994 is seen to be unprecedented. As Barnett wrote, "For the statistically inclined, the rate works out to be 333 deaths per hour, 5 deaths per minute ... [t]he Rwandan genocide has the macabre distinction of exceeding the rate of killing attained during the Holocaust" (Barnett 2002:1). Consequently, this not only reduces human suffering to relative questions of scale, but presumes that such comparisons are in some way meaningful.

But the essential reason why the Rwandan genocide is seen as unique is that there existed both the foreknowledge of, and a capacity to prevent it. Rwanda has come to represent one of the most ignominious and abject moral failures of the United Nations. UNAMIR is understood to have provided sufficient forewarning of the genocide. After the genocide began, the Security Council refused to countenance intervention, even though such intervention would have been relatively unproblematic. The only significant response on the part of the Security Council was to authorize the withdrawal of the bulk of UNAMIR. In short, the Rwandan population were abandoned with full United

Nations knowledge of what was occurring. As a consequence, culpability for this failure is seen to lie with the Security Council and the Secretariat, certain 'Western Nations,' or even more ambiguously the 'international community' or humanity itself. At its most strident, the failure to intervene is equated with actual 'complicity' in the genocide (Melvern 2000:5).

With little variation, this 'uniqueness' has become the predominate understanding of the Rwandan genocide, one that dominates both academic discourse and the general perception of what happened. Indicative of the way that genocide is treated as a discrete object of study, Rwanda has come to be known solely because of the genocide, and it is through the genocide alone that Rwanda continues to be understood. While this may reflect the reality confronting many Rwandans given the inestimable consequences of what happened, the attention paid to the genocide and the desire to uphold the uniqueness of what occurred in Rwanda has created an implicit conceptual bias. This bias privileges the 'one hundred days' of the genocide, and has resulted in a decontextualisation of what occurred in Rwanda both before and after 1994.

The ongoing attribution of uniqueness to the Rwandan genocide depends on an idealisation of the role played by the 'West,' as well as on generalised abstractions about the nature of what occurred in Rwanda. Yet, the acute moral and historical questions raised by the extent of the killing can only be answered by reference to what happened in Rwanda immediately after the RPF invasion in 1990 that precipitated the genocide. Treatment of the Rwandan genocide as unique ignores not only the intrinsic historical redundancy this raises (as any event can be accorded such status), but also that such killing and extensive cruelty is present where impunity is guaranteed (Kimonyo 2000: 4; Kagabo 1995).

In many ways, what occurred in Rwanda is consistently seen to invoke questions regarding both the nature of humanity, and who it is that qualifies as a human being worthy of being saved. This reflects the tendency to invest the concept of genocide with such deontological significance, that Rwanda now "haunt[s] the collective history of humanity" (Verhofstadt 2000). Acceding to the view that genocide has a singular and unique status affirms the hierarchy that has been created within the Rwandan population itself, where there is special recognition of a select number considered as genocide 'survivors' – or *rescapés* - but not of those who were killed in the course of the war and in years after 1994. The urgent concern for the suffering of the genocide survivors that characterises such projects as 'Remembering Rwanda,' ignores the fact that the killing in Rwanda was not limited to the 'one hundred days' of the genocide, but encompassed the Democratic Republic of Congo, Rwanda itself and Burundi.

Consequently, treating the Rwandan genocide in such a way derives from an aesthetic affection, where the full extent of what has occurred after 1994 is either wittingly or unwittingly ignored. The affective response to the Rwandan genocide that now predominates, disregards that it was the war itself that was central to the genocide occurring. It has created an implicit conceptual bias, one that does not consider the subsequent violence in Rwanda as part of the same historical phenomenon. Although couched in the language of reconciliation and acceptance of culpability - or for the Belgian Prime Minister, Guy Verhofsdtat in 2000, an explicit desire for 'forgiveness' (Verhofstadt 2000) - continued emphasis on the uniqueness of the Rwandan genocide and the failure to prevent it is inimical to understanding and appreciating what has occurred in Rwanda. Yet, more significantly, the desire to commemorate and preserve the memory of the genocide through such projects as 'Remembering Rwanda' neglects the way it has become subject to a concerted ideological campaign by the RPF. Since 1994, the RPF have astutely created and sustained a 'politically correct'(International Crisis Group 2002: 1) view of the genocide, one that excludes any consideration of their responsibility.

In effect, the perceived urgency of the need to preserve the memory of the genocide through such projects as 'Remembering Rwanda' coincides with the way the RPF has revised Rwandan history to legitimise their rule. Both the years following the RPF invasion in 1990 and the pre-colonial history of Rwanda are seen in the light of the RPF struggle to liberate all Rwandans. Essentially, this is seen as a struggle to free Rwanda from the divisions introduced by colonial racialisation of Tutsi and Hutu, as well as the struggle against dictatorship and corruption that has plagued Rwanda since independence. Accordingly, the 1994 genocide is constructed as simply a culmination of these aspects of Rwandan society, which have finally been overcome with the RPF's victory. In the same vein as 'Remembering Rwanda,' memory preservation is central to preserving the knowledge of the genocide so it is not repeated in Rwanda.

But the genocide has become the central aspect of a coherent ideology that is used to obfuscate the extent of the RPF's killings in 1994, and to consolidate their rule following their victory in 1994. From the correspondence of their representatives to the UN, as well as from numerous press releases and statements, it is readily apparent that the RPF leadership were aware that the ignominy of the UN's failure would serve both to justify their victory and to legitimize any subsequent actions taken to consolidate their rule. Even before the end of the war in July, this realisation allowed the RPF to increasingly "convert its moral superiority into [an] analytic monopoly" (Pottier 2002: 177). The initial moral superiority enjoyed by the RPF was conferred through their conscious decision to utilize the genocide (or more specifically the putative 'failure' to prevent it) as a means of legitimizing their rule internationally. This was aided by widespread ignorance about Rwanda in the years prior to 1994.

Those who came to Rwanda after 1994 could observe not only the devastating effects of the genocide and immense scale of the killing, but also the willingness of the RPF to offer a convincing and readily understandable account of what had happened. The 'Government of National Unity' sworn-in in July 1994 attempted to represent a new beginning for Rwanda, and included members of all political parties not involved in the genocide. Its members, both Hutu and Tutsi, were those who had aligned themselves with the RPF prior to the death of Habyarimana. Consequently, the 'Government of National Unity' was seen as a continuation of the political liberalisation process begun in 1992, one that the organisers of the genocide had hoped to prevent. Also frequently commented on were the disciplined soldiers of the RPF, who, having grown up in Uganda, were able to speak English and therefore could communicate easily with the vast number of journalists and humanitarian workers who came to Rwanda. Due to the mass return of those who had been refugees since Rwandan independence thirty years previously, the vast number of those who had fled the RPF advance, as well as the immense number killed, there was little indication of what the situation in Rwanda was like prior to the genocide and the war.

In the absence of any dissenting understanding of what caused the genocide (except for the patent racial mythologising and propaganda of the self proclaimed 'Rwandan Government in Exile' – a continuation of the 'Interim Government' that organised the genocide), the ideal of neutrality and impartiality after the genocide was, according to Philip Gourevitch (1995), not only irrelevant but also morally repulsive. Combined with what was seen as the direct result of the 'West's' callous indifference, a moral legitimacy was conferred onto the RPF and the 'Government of National Unity' almost reflexively. Read simply, the failure of the Security Council to authorize UNAMIR to intervene not only allowed the genocide to occur - which according to Paul Kagame was due to "complicity more than ignorance" (Gourevitch 1996: 185) - it was the RPF alone that effectively put an end to the genocide by defeating the Interim Government. These two aspects of what occurred in Rwanda, the indifference to the genocide and the RPF's subsequent victory in the war, are now widely perceived as almost synonymous. The 'war of liberation' begun in 1990 by the RPF, became in 1994 a war to stop genocide, and they continue to be seen as the "only force that had a chance to stop the genocide" (Barnett 2002: 15). Much of what Peter Uvin (2001: 76) describes as "the explosion of writing" and has "become something of a cottage industry" (Lang 2002: 143) on the Rwanda genocide, has relied on interviews with RPF members to build a case for the remonstrating the 'West.' In this writing, there is a sense of the RPF's self aggrandizement, and an awareness that in the years since the genocide, the efficacy of the organization's 'moral superiority' in courting sympathy and an uncritical acceptance of the RPF's version of the genocide has not been lost. Linda Melvern (2000: 189) for example, whose work attempts to expose the 'betrayal' by the 'West', quotes Paul Kagame; "All those claiming to be civilised had turned their backs, ...I knew that we were alone".

It is here that the convergence between Rwanda's history as promoted by the RPF and the implicit decontextualisation of the events of 1994 is most apparent. The inauguration of RPF rule after the genocide was seen as a radical break from divisive policies that had been in place since independence. With the RPF having been imbued with 'moral sympathy' due to their previous isolation, the ideology of reconciliation and national unity they promoted was understood as the only rational and viable alternative for Rwandan society. The moral sympathy already extended to the RPF by virtue of stopping the genocide, then extended to sympathy for their attempt to establish reconciliation in the face of the absolute collapse of Rwandan society. Given the vast moral questions seemingly invoked by the presence of genocide, the question of reconciliation after such an event carries similar weight. By overcoming the division between Tutsi and Hutu through abolition of any mention of racial affiliation on identity cards, installing a government that consisted of both Hutu and Tutsi ostensibly based on the 1993 Arusha Accords that demonstrated a commitment to democracy, and by describing reconciliation as the basis for a new Rwanda, the future of a 'new Rwanda' had been ushered in with the RPF's victory.

Consequently, the problems confronting the new administration were interpreted as problems arising directly from the 'three months' of the genocide. The most important questions about what had occurred in Rwanda were limited to the genocide itself, as the immediate problems facing Rwandan society were implicitly resolved by 'moral superiority' and the ultimate beneficence of the RPF. Any criticism that was voiced of the new regime was seen in the context of the effects of the genocide on Rwanda. Combined with their readiness to explain the situation solely by reference to the genocide, this criticism did not detract from the inherent legitimacy of the RPF, simply because of the enormity of what confronted them.

In years after 1994, the genocide has come to be portrayed as the defining moment in Rwandan history; a culmination of the divisive practices of colonization that were carried on through independence and continued by the Habyarimana regime. With the RPF's victory, 'liberation' had been finally achieved, which permitted a return to an unproblematic and idealized Rwandan national identity. Yet while there was a mass exodus of refugees who fled from the war and the RPF advance, the circumstances of those Rwandans who remained inside Rwanda displayed "a chilling continuity" (Wagner 1998: 30) with the previous months of war and genocide. Although the genocide in the form of a concerted policy of the 'Interim Government' ended with the RPF's installation on 18 July 1994 of their own 'Government of National Unity', the killing throughout Rwanda did not. When the RPF finally came to power in July, there was a tendency for its members to call 'meetings.' At these meetings, generally anyone who held a position of authority, who was young and male, or in some cases, every person who attended the meeting, was killed. These meetings became so frequent that in Kinyarwanda, to meet together *kwitaba inama* became known as *kwitaba imana.* (*Imana* is the Kinyarwanda word for God, and to die can be roughly translated 'to meet God'). Although the evidence for these abuses by the RPF was initially difficult to document owing to the new government's strict control of movement, it is certain now that they were both extensive and deliberate.

The lack of prior knowledge of Rwanda among most journalists and commentators was compensated for by the willingness of members of the RPF to cooperate in providing an easily apprehended explanation for what had happened. As Johann Pottier (2002) argues, most of the new myths about Rwandan history originate here, through the combination of naivety and horror about what had just occurred. In a similar manner to the massacres that occurred in Burundi in 1972 and 1988, the RPF engaged in the killing of any potential opposition while consolidating control throughout Rwanda. In the years after the genocide, there followed the repeated massacres of refugees who had fled from the RPF advance into Eastern Zaire in 1996.

Either ignored or alluded to in passing, as though the killing was to be expected following such a thing as genocide, this continuity is marginal to current understandings of Rwanda. Yet, it is essential not only for an understanding of the new opposition groups that have formed in exile, but for appreciation of the way that the genocide itself has been "put to service in the interests of a powerful minority" (Brauman et al 2000: 155). Centring around the RPF, this minority consists largely of those who lived as refugees in Uganda, and whose concerns are tied up with the business and economic interests of the new regime. While the Rwandan genocide has become a discrete object of study, having now been placed alongside other instances of genocide, within Rwanda itself there is a discrepancy between the way it has been utilised and promoted and the actual living conditions of those who survived. Despite the disavowal by the RPF of the divisions between Hutu and Tutsi that have beset Rwanda, the genocide continues to be deployed as a means of legitimizing their rule. The continued emphasis on the genocide through annual commemoration ceremonies reiterates the unspoken "eternal culpability" (Brauman 2000: 155) of the Hutu within Rwanda. Similarly, the victims of the genocide are defined through a corporatist understanding of 'Tutsi.' The group set up to represent the survivors of the genocide, *Ibuka*, itself funded by and aligned with the current Rwandan government, released a statement in 1999 saying that the Rwandan genocide should be named 'The Tutsi genocide'. Despite the unity and reconciliation that is the ostensible goal of the 'Government of National Unity,' construing the genocide as one solely of the Tutsi excludes not only all those Hutu who were killed trying to save Tutsi, but also those who refused to participate, and those killed by the RPF.

While the genocide continues to be equated with the corporatist view of Tutsi identity, in that all Tutsi inside Rwanda were threatened after April 1994, it presupposes that the Tutsi themselves represent a unified group. But those who fled Rwanda following the violence surrounding independence in 1962 had radically different experiences to those who remained in Rwanda. Immediately after independence, the repeated and unsuccessful attempts by the former Tutsi monarchy to overthrow the new government led to reprisal killings of those Tutsi who had stayed in Rwanda. Despite the knowledge that these invasions would lead to further killings, they continued to place those Tutsi inside of Rwanda at risk.

According to Filip Reyntjens (1997), despite the limited opportunities offered by the Habyarimana regime, Tutsi within Rwanda welcomed its 1973 coup. From 1973 until 1990 there was no violence directed towards the Tutsi population, and the question of identity itself had become "archaic" (Nationale Assemblé 1998: 31). It was immediately apparent after the RPF's 1990 invasion that the Tutsi inside Rwanda would once again suffer recriminations as had happened less than thirty years earlier. Yet, what is also frequently expressed both by the Rwandan Government and such projects as 'Remembering Rwanda,' is the notion that the genocide started in 1959, just before Rwandan independence. This claim of historical continuity amongst the Tutsi serves to obscure the knowledge that by launching the invasion, the RPF were aware that they were putting the Tutsi population inside of Rwanda once again at risk. Consequently, treatment of the genocide as one of Tutsi alone, "biases the genocide by attributing a moral superiority [to the government] while the victims of the genocide were often the poor Tutsi peasants and the government was formed essentially by former exiles who were never physically threatened" (Prunier 1997).

Aware of the previous ignorance about Rwanda, and the tendency to accord genocide such aesthetic significance, when they took control of Rwanda in July 1994, the RPF began to "preserve the memory of the genocide", and to accord those killed "the dignity of memory and truth" (Republic of Rwanda 1995: 26,29). Initially, this consisted of leaving undisturbed the remains of those killed at the numerous massacre sites throughout Rwanda. The establishment of more permanent memorials began in 1997, with both the exhumation and display of skeletal remains. In Gigonkoro, the desire to preserve the supposed physical evidence was such that bodies were exhumed from their mass graves in order to be displayed. To stave off the process of decay, the remains were cleaned and treated chemically. Subsequently, they were laid out and displayed inside the school (Lauras 1997; Kayigamba 1997). Although this practice has generally been understood as a unique and fitting response to the preservation of the memory of genocide, a similar display of corpses and skeletal remains exists in Uganda (Associated Press 1986; 1988). It is difficult to establish whether the RPF deliberately adopted the same policy as Yoweri Museveni or whether the decision was a continuation of their previous experiences under Museveni. Yet unlike the memorial sites in Uganda, which have declining significance, and no longer serve to justify the NRA's war, in Rwanda these memorial sites have attained an iconic status. Not only are they intended to reinforce the ultimate legitimacy of the RPF's struggle against the Habyarimana dictatorial regime, but also to serve as a reminder of the international indifference to the genocide. Considering how frequently these memorial sites have been visited, and how frequently they have been described in the numerous written accounts of the genocide, it seems that the policy of maintaining these sites has thus far been effective.

Although the massacre sites are often seen as the ultimate symbolic representation of the Rwandan genocide, in that nothing else can more 'poignantly' demonstrate the reality of what occurred in 1994, they in effect exist solely to provide an opportunity for 'reflection' (in whatever form) for foreigners. Few Rwandans themselves have either the means or the desire to visit these sites. The policy of 'memory preservation,' is limited practically to the few foreign visitors to Rwanda.

Coinciding with the discernable policy directed towards outsiders consolidated around these few 'memorial sites', each anniversary of the genocide is commemorated in ceremonies held throughout Rwanda. Beginning on 7 April, the date seen to mark the beginning of the genocide (and the day following the killing of the then-Rwandan President, Juvenal Habyarimana), the week long genocide commemoration ceremonies consist of extensive radio and television programmes dedicated solely to the genocide. Throughout the week of commemoration, or 'mourning,' graphic news footage, documentaries, and specially composed songs are repeatedly broadcast. Even more necessary to the anniversary ceremonies is the reburial in newly consecrated mass graves of exhumed remains, which serve to memorialize the genocide as the defining event in Rwandan history. During these reburial ceremonies, a speech is given by the President which stresses the distinction between the divisive practices of the Habyarimana regime that led to the genocide, and the unity which has become a possibility for Rwanda since then.

The theme of Rwandan unity also continues throughout the week of commemoration in local meetings held at various administrative levels, which generally involve discussions about the question of the colonial construction of the Hutu/Tutsi division that ultimately led to the genocide. Combined with a new flag and national anthem adopted in 2001, as well as the removal of agricultural implements from the Rwandan national symbols (as these were seen to be the main weapons used to carry out the genocide), the intensive process of memorialisation suggests that the genocide remains an inveterate feature of life in Rwanda, and is what Rwanda has now come to be known for worldwide. The emphasis on the genocide through these ceremonies does not represent the extreme individual suffering for those who lived through the months of genocide and years of war, but represents an event that is vital to a sense of national identity. This sense of identity remains contingent upon the genocide. Yet whether these commemorations have the desired "beneficial effect" (IBUKA) for the survivors of the genocide is hard to ascertain.

Despite the difficulty in appreciating the situation for those who survived both the war and the genocide, the continued reference to the 'genocide memorial sites' set up by the RPF epitomises the decontextualisation of what occurred in Rwanda. Phillip Gourevitch's (1998) book, *We Wish to Inform You that Tomorrow We will be Killed with our Families,* not only met with critical acclaim, but its publication was fortuitous. By then it had become widely recognised that the UN had failed to uphold the Genocide Convention. Both Kofi Annan and Bill Clinton had acknowledged this failure, invoking the culpability of not just the United Nations, but also of all humanity for failing to intervene to stop the genocide. In his book, Gourevitch describes a visit to Nyarubyue, in the south west of Rwanda, one of the main 'memorial sites'. The bodies of those killed had been left there under the orders of the RPF. When Gourevitch (1998: 19) arrived in late 1995, he described both his motivation for the visit and the scene that confronted him:

> Perhaps in examining this extremity with me, you hope for some understanding, some insight, some flicker of self-knowledge – a moral, a lesson, or a clue about how to behave in this world: some such information. I don't discount the possibility, but when it comes to genocide, you already know right from wrong. The best reason I have come up with for looking closely into Rwanda's stories is that ignoring them makes me even more uncomfortable about existence and my place in it. The horror, as horror, interests me only insofar as a precise memory of the offence is necessary to understand its legacy. The dead at Nyarubye [a memorial site in Kibungo province] were, I'm afraid, beautiful.

Even though there was evidence emerging about the nature of the RPF rule in Rwanda from as early as 1995, they still enjoy an unprecedented uncritical acceptance internationally. Gourevitch's belief that "when it comes to genocide, you already know right from wrong," forms the basis for much of this acceptance. The absence of critique about the way these memorial sites have become the focus of international attention is evidence of the aesthetic affection that has come to predominate discourse about Rwanda. Aware of this tendency, the RPF has been able to cultivate a representation of the genocide that precludes their own responsibility in what occurred. This also allows the continuing refusal of the RPF to acknowledge that their invasion in 1990 precipitated the genocide. Filip Reyntjens (1997) believes that not only are the RPF "politically co-responsible" for the genocide, but that the extent of their own crimes, both during the war and after the genocide, is immense. Given the lack of any substantial critique of the 'Remembering Rwanda' project so far, and of the planned commemoration ceremonies for 2004, it seems that the

RPF's policy of exploiting the way genocide is understood has succeeded. While genocide did occur in Rwanda, intrinsic to the RPF's success in marginalizing their own abuses is the aesthetic affection with which Rwanda is now interpreted. In contrast to the urgent need to preserve the memory of the Rwandan genocide as a means of reconciliation, questions of impunity and historical objectivity would seem to matter little. "Without compassion and rehabilitation for all the victims, without judgement of the authors of these two categories of crimes, there exists little chance of fighting against impunity, and little chance of reconciliation"(Gasana and Nsengimana 1999: 1-5).

References

Barnett, M. (2002) *Eyewitness to a Genocide: the United Nations and Rwanda,* London: Cornell University Press.

Brauman, R., Smith, S. & Vidal, C. (2000) 'Politique de Terreur et Privilège D'impunité au Rwanda', *Esprit,* pp. 266-267.

Gasana, J. & Nsengimana, N. (1999) *Contributions au combat contre le negationnisme of génocide et la delation politique,* Lausanne, Juin.

Gourevitch, P. (1995) 'After the Genocide', *The New Yorker,* 18 December.

Gourevtich, P. (1996) 'After Genocide; A Conversation with Paul Kagame', *Transition,* 72.

Gourevitch, P. (1998) *We wish to Inform you that Tomorrow we will be Killed with our Families: Stories from Rwanda,* New York: Farrar Straus & Giroux.

IBUKA, "La précarité des conditions de vie des rescapes du genocide au Rwanda": http://www.ibuka.org/fra/rescapes.htm

International Crisis Group (2002) *Fin de transition au Rwanda: Une libéralisation politique nécessaire,* ICG Rapport Afrique N°53, 13 novembre.

Kagabo, J. (1995) 'Après le génocide: notes de voyage', *Temps Moderne,* 583(50).

Kaplan, G. (2003) 'Rwanda Commemorates its "Forgotten" Genocide', *Agence France-Presse*, 8 April.

Jean Baptiste Kayigamba, J-B. (1997) 'Rwanda: Communities Turning Churches into Shrines', *Inter Press Service*, 16 September.

Kimonyo, J-P.. *Revue Critique des Interprétations du Conflit Rwandais,* Editions de l'univerisite nationale du Rwanda: Butare.

Lang, A. (2002) 'Global Governance and Genocide in Rwanda', *Ethics and International Affairs*, 16(1), pp.143-150.

Lauras, D. (1997) 'Rwanda Preserves Bodies of 1994 Genocide Victims for Memorial', *Agence France-Presse*, 25 July.

Melvern, L. (2000) *A People Betrayed: the Role of the West in Rwanda's Genocide* London: Zed Books.

Nationale Assemblé, (1998) *La Mission d'information de la Commission sur Rwanda: sommaire des comptes rendues d'auditions du 24 mars 1998 au 5 mai 1998: Audition de M. André Guichaoua.*

Pottier, J. (2002) *Re-Imagining Rwanda: Conflict, Survival and Disinformation in the Late Twentieth Century,* Cambridge University Press: Cambridge.

Prunier, M. (1997) *Compte rendu analytique des auditions: Mercredi 11 juin 1997*, Commission d'enquête concernant les événements du Rwanda, Senat de Belgique, Session Ordinaire, 1996-1997.

Remembering Rwanda,http://www.visiontv.ca/Remember Rwanda/main_pf.htm

Republic of Rwanda. (1995) Recommendations of the Conference held in Kigal from November 1st to 5th 1995 on 'Genocide, Impunity and Accountibility: Dialogue for a National and International Response', Kigali: Office of the President.

Reyntjens, F. (1997) quoted in "Tutsi-led Party Shares Blame for Tutsi Genocide: Witness." *Agence France-Presse*, 14 October.

Uvin, P. (2002) 'Reading the Rwandan Genocide', *International Studies Review*, 3(3), pp. 75-99.

van Leeuwen, M. (2001) 'Rwanda's Imidugudu Programme and Earlier Experiences with Villiagisation and Resettlement in East Africa', *The Journal of Modern African Studies*, 39(4) pp. 623-644.

Verhofstadt, G, (2000) Discours du Premier Ministre Guy Verhofstadt à l'occasion de la commémoration du 6e anniversaire du début du Génocide rwandais, Kigali le 7 avril 2000: http://premier.fgov.be/topics/speeches/f_speech12.html

Wagner, M. (1998) 'All the 'Bourgmestre's' Men: Making Sense of the Genocide in Rwanda', *Africa Today*, 45(1), pp. 25-37.

Associated Press (1986) "Museveni Leads Tour Of Site Of Alleged Atrocities", 11 February 1986.

Associated Press (1988) "Uganda Collects Skulls and Bones of Massacre Victims", 20 April 1988.

Chapter 6

Global Impulses/Local Politics: Comparing Two Eras of Constitution-Making in Kenya

Edith Miguda

Do current globalisation trends spell out an era of 'post-ethnicity'? This chapter argues that given the current globalising trends, ethnicity as a central basis for cleavage formation in local politics is weakening. New forms of interactions between global forces and local events have emerged in Africa, inspiring alternative forms of coalition and cleavage among citizens. In making this argument, I examine two eras of constitution making in Kenya associated with different manifestations of global trends; the Independence Constitution era that ended in 1963, and the major constitutional review process that began in 2000[1]. I argue that the global and local forces that led to constitutional changes associated with decolonisation in the 1960s, ushered in forces that oriented Kenya to play its role on the global stage.

Currently, the global forces and local interactions that urge constitutional changes associated with democratisation, impel Kenya to make global consensus work locally. In this regard, there has been a shift in emphasis from globalising the local that was important during the decolonisation period to that of localising the global that is pre-eminent in the current constitutional review environment. With this shift, ethnicity as the central factor in cleavage formation has been weakened, thus reducing its hegemonic role in explaining local events, given the rise of newer bases of group formation.

This shift has, in part, been deployed by what I term *global impulses,* that are the emission of particular forces, from particular sources, that generate power and change as they enter and move into specific local contexts. Drawing on the themes of globalisation enables one to examine the shifts in the continued interconnectedness of people through sharing and shared ideas, values and discourses. The term *global impulses* depicts ideas, discourses, and contexts that emanate from a variety of global centres and interact with local forces to generate change. The idea that the global and local mutually constitute each other enables us to examine ethnicity within a larger frame than in its local context (see Barker,1995; and Featherstone,1995). Importantly, this analysis leads to an examination of *post-ethnicity* in order to draw from the wider discourses on 'post' studies - postcolonialism, postmodernism and so on - that have expanded frontiers of thought; particularly the argument that the contemporary world is one in which individual identities are increasingly cross-cultural and one where values are increasingly relative (Chabel 1996). I adopt the usage of 'post' to ethnicity in order to expand the frontiers around which we can examine the interplay between ethnicity and other forces of history.

Comparing Trends in Two Eras of Constitution Making in Kenya

Globalisation has been going on since the mid 15th Century. In the 18th Century it was a combination of global impulses that led to the colonisation of Africa by European nations. By the mid 20th Century, global impulses interacting with local forces necessitated the constitutional changes leading to decolonisation. In the post-Cold War period, and after 30 years of independence in many African nations, more recent global impulses, influenced by the dynamics of globalisation, have urged moves towards democratisation and good governance through constitutional change. These distinct yet related, periods of global impulses impacting upon Africa can be demonstrated by examining Kenya's current constitutional review process. This is not the first time that global and local forces have converged to impel constitutional changes in the country. Between 1940 and 1963, Kenya underwent a process of constitutional debate and change that culminated in the Independence constitutional arrangement of 1963.

The Independence Constitution derived from global impulses interacting with local politics that were played out both inside Kenya and in the UK, at Lancaster House where the independence of Kenya was negotiated. The constitutional events and engagements drew from global impulses emanating from such diverse locations as America, Egypt, Southern and Central Africa, India, and the USSR among others (Odinga 1967). Global impulses, flowing via specific discourses of self-determination, interacted with local forces resisting colonial exploitation to force a crafting of alternative, competing, constitutions that represented various interests in colonial Kenya. The debates and disagreements that manifested in competing constitutional proposals finally led to the three constitutional conferences at Lancaster House[2]. The Independence Constitution gave rise to the current Constitution, which has been under official review since 2000. This Constitution, however, had been under scrutiny almost from the time of its inception. During the presidencies of Jomo Kenyatta (the first President of Kenya from 1963-1978) and Daniel Arap Moi (the second President of Kenya from 1978-2002), both leaders moulded the issues that currently populate the constitutional review process. In the 1980s and early 1990s, a burgeoning and vocal civil society became the agents that generated constitutional debates, while human rights discourse served as a significant framework around which constitutional issues were initiated and debated.

There are a number of significant parallels in the global and local interactions that propelled constitution making in Kenya in the two eras. The current comprehensive review of the Constitution draws from a history of a number of constitutional amendments that vested unchecked powers on the presidency and in turn, led citizens to call for constitutional changes that would enable power sharing, checks and balances and greater citizen participation in the 'making of Kenya'. Similarly, the same issues of power and control were at the centre of the controversies surrounding the Independence Constitution. Constitutional debates at that time drew from a colonial constitutional legacy that had vested much power in settlers at the expense of other racial groups. This ignited demands for constitutional changes that would address many of the issues around representation and control of the state.

From a global perspective, both constitution making eras have taken place within the context of major global upheavals. In the first era, a war weary world, in the post-Second World War period, sent global impulses urging decolonisation and, thus, the establishment of the first Independence Constitution. In the current era of constitution making, the post-Cold War period has produced global impulses urging democratisation and good governance. In a rather significant way, both the Independence Constitution and the current constitutional review process hold definite roles in positioning Kenya to function in a global system. On the one hand, the constitutional arrangements through which Kenya became independent meant that Kenya would have the opportunity to perform among the other independent nations of the world. One of the immediate actions after independence was an application for membership to the United Nations through which Kenya became a member of the UN "just hours after attaining independence" in December 1963 (Kenya and the United Nations, www.un.int/kenya/kenya_un.htm).

Global Impulses, Ethnicity and The Independence Constitution.

Colonial administrative structures, institutions and practices both invented and established 'ethnicity' as the single most significant context of political interest (Berman 1998). Ethnicity was invented as young men and women grew from the womb of old Africa into the early colonial Africa (Odhiambo-Atieno 2000). From this legacy, Kenya's Independence Constitution was negotiated within the context of global impulses and local demands that coupled constitution making and constitutional change to ethnic demands. First, the Independence Constitution was debated in a global era that demanded the rights of peoples to choose the form of government they themselves deemed representative of their aspirations. With the formation of the UN in 1945, Kenyan nationalists sought independence from British colonial rule within the global paradigm of the rights of all peoples to self-determination. However, the colonial government had constituted Africans along 'tribal' and 'ethnic' lines. Consequently, different groups, arranged along ethnic cleavages, assumed different standpoints towards the proposed constitutional changes aimed at self-determination. From specific ethnic standpoints, groups in turn proposed competing, alternative constitutions that resulted in disagreements, bargains and negotiations in order to arrive at a final constitutional arrangement which would accommodate Kenya's ethnic equation.

It is significant that the initial constitutional hitches arose from parameters framed by the racial questions and race relations of the day, which pitched various racial groups in Kenya against each other. From its inception, the colonial administration placed various groups in a hierarchy of racial privileges, rights, and status in politics and economic and social life. Leys (1975) describes how European settlers, for example, maintained racial supremacy and privileges through a monopoly of high-potential land, agricultural labour, government services and the most profitable crops. Africans, at the opposite extreme in the racial divide, lived under appalling conditions in poor and congested reserves and overcrowded urban centres, with poor or no government services, and were subjected to extremely poor working conditions.

Joseph (1997) points out that under racial hierarchies, constitutional debates are often limited to demanding the same rights and privileges other races possess, or to its corollary of removing constraints on lesser privileged racial groups. Indeed as the constitutional debates raged in Kenya in the 1950s, racial tensions were drawn into conflicts around the Constitution that pitched European settlers, Africans, Asians and Arabs as racial groups in opposing and contentious positions with regard to their location in any constitutional arrangement[3].

The settler's demands centred around continued European dominance in Kenya. This was part of an earlier and wider global enterprise aimed at enforcing Anglo supremacy[4]. However, the Kenyan variant of European supremacy had taken a local flavour since the European occupation, as settlers became 'declassed' and assumed an overall racial privilege in Kenya. Frost (1997) describes the composition of settlers as including blacksmiths, shoemakers, Afrikaners running from depression and hardship that arose due to the Boer War, as well as those from the aristocracy with money and social position. In spite of the mix, the European settlers took on privileges and assumed status that a number of them did not ordinarily enjoy in their own countries. A memo by sir Donald Cameron (1927) lamented that,

> [w]here native labour is available, Europeans even of the domestic class refuse to perform for themselves the services which they were forced to discharge for themselves in their own country.

Such a symbolic assumption of supremacy was accompanied by demands for greater rights and privileges within the colony in relation to African and other racial groups. By 1945, these rights were deeply entrenched and the settlers, through their party (the Electors' Union), aimed at preserving these rights and privileges at all costs including the use of military force to resist any constitutional change that did not guarantee their privileged status.[5] A note from Mr. Hugh Fraser for example, described some Europeans as "once more carrying constitutions inside their pistol holsters" (Fraser, The Kenya Constitutional Question: A Note. PRO CO 822/599). In addition to demands within Kenya, the Electors' Union also mobilized opinion externally, drawing from global impulses and urging local inclinations into the global scene[6].

In their search for European supremacy at all costs, the settlers were completely indifferent to African political aspirations, and adopted an uncompromising racial attitude that brought white aspirations into a direct collision course with African nationalism (Ogot 2000: 65). The collision was to cause a local political split among Europeans[7] during which race was translated into ethnicity as Europeans became 'tribalised' and joined local tribes in opposing or advocating specific constitutional arrangements[8].

The colonial government was another source for the global impulses entrenching ethnicity as the central locus of cleavage during the constitutional debates. The Colonial Office in particular began to view Kenya not just through the prism of race, but also through the prism of 'tribe', as ethnicity began to figure more prominently in imperial calculations (Maxon 2000: 46).

The Asians formed a separate racial group with neither the privileges of the white colonizers or the under-privileges of the Africans. Yet, their constitutional politics, like that of the Europeans and that of the Africans, had a global derivation as well as a local flavour. With origins in India and the connections between India and Britain, Asians in Kenya held the rather precarious comparative racial position of a 'privileged/disadvantaged' group. They initially had a nominated representation in the legislative council, but were later enfranchised to elect representatives to this council through a common communal roll. Throughout the colonial period, settlers continuously resisted political concessions to Indians, and they often got their way[9]. When the constitutional debates began, European settlers drew from this legacy and locally expressed sentiments against constitutional concessions to Indians[10]. Indians on the other hand were the envy of other racial groups, particularly the Arabs and the Somalis. The former sought equal treatment and status with the Indians while the latter sought racial identity parity with Indians[11]. In the racial equation in Kenya, the next in line after Indians were the Arabs and

Somalis. Arabs stated that they represented the Arab immigrants from Arabia, demanded that they be distinguished from natives, and protested against criminal procedures, ordinances and other colonial statutes that included Arabs and Somalis as natives[12]. Indeed the official definition of 'native' had a clause that excluded Somali and Swahili.

Within this racial equation, the original imperial vision, predominant since 1942, was to find people who could be bound to Britain in such a way that they would protect and maintain British economic and strategic interests in Kenya (Maxon 2000: 46). Along these lines, and coupled with the increasing demands by Africans for greater representation and 'Africa for Africans', the colonial government worked around initiatives on multiculturalism[13]. Although Africans and moderate European settlers used the multicultural proposals to stake out concessions[14], by the late 1950s both Africans and radical Europeans vehemently opposed multiculturalism as an option for Kenya. These objections finally forced the colonial government to adopt a policy aimed at scraping multiculturalism and pursuing a rapid policy change towards African majority rule[15].

Once the colonial government abandoned multiculturalism as a constitutional option, ethnicity took centre stage as the locus of constitutional bargaining and negotiation. As noted earlier, within Kenya Europeans became 'tribalised' while the Colonial Office convinced itself that tribalism and ethnicity were the factors to reckon with in Kenya's politics. Among the Africans, ethnic divisions became glaring as ethnic interests emerged as a common feature of decolonisation (Murungi 1995). Ethnicity framed demands for constitutional safeguards for the interests of 'minority' groups. Ethnicity and ethnic tensions held up constitutional talks in London, as disagreements pitched various ethnic groups against each other leading to both internal and interracial splits, coalitions and counter-coalitions among groups with competing ethnic agendas and visions for constitutional change.

Ethnicity not only became the central identity divide, but also the central locus of configuring interests. 'Minority' ethnic groups bargained from the position of fear that the larger ethnic groups would dominate independent Kenya. Their desire through the Kenya African Democratic Union (KADU) was to have a constitution that would protect their interests as minority groups in Kenya. The settlers approached the constitution from a fear that their dominant position would come to an end and wanted a constitution that would protect their interests as a minority. They joined forces with the smaller African ethnic groups on a commonality founded upon fear. The larger ethnic groups wanted 'independence now' in order to acquire the necessary power to rule Kenya. In the midst of these local politics, global impulses, in particular those flowing from pressure by the United States and the Soviet Union, independent African states, and African nationalists travelling or studying abroad, also sent renewed impetus for decolonisation.

With these ethnic tensions and conflicts present in the 1960s, a new Constitution was debated, negotiated and finally agreed upon within the framework of fear and desires to protect threatened ethnic group interests. In the final analysis, the Majimbo Constitution[16] that ushered in independence in 1963 sealed ethnicity as the central locus of political competition, and cleavage formation in the political system of independent Kenya by passing Lower House constituencies and Upper House seats almost exclusively along ethnic lines. Ogendo (2001) concluded that political parties reached independence as little more than federated ethnic loyalties, grouped around individual personalities.

The Current Constitutional Review process: Decentring Ethnicity

Justifying the need for a comprehensive review of the Constitution, the Constitution of Kenya Review Commission (CKRC) stated that attempts to accommodate everyone's interests in the Independence Constitution necessitated an approach resulting in inherent instability (Ojwang 1990). Speaking from hindsight, with a clearer picture of the unfolding myriad of constitutional amendments since independence, a number of Kenyan scholars have pointed out that the Independence Constitution was untenable for a number of reasons. It was too complicated, and, according to the CKRC, showed a remarkable distrust of power. The Constitution was alien to the history of government in Kenya and at variance with the authoritarian structure of the administrative structures inherited from the colonial period (Ogende 2001). At the same time, none of the signatories had any faith in it (Munene 2001). These sentiments are particularly significant in understanding some of the modalities of interaction between global forces and local politics.

By the time of the first anniversary of independence, constitutional amendments were initiated as a practice that has since seen an average rate of one constitutional amendment per year (Muigai 2001). The frequent amendments to the Constitution resulted in extensive presidential powers that enabled large abuses of power by the presidents of Kenya[17]. The first group of amendments removed, and finally wiped out, regionalism as designed in the Independence Constitution, creating instead a situation that the Kenya African National Union (KANU) would have liked to see in 1963[18]. In 1964 KADU dissolved and members joined KANU. However, this occurred without any clear crafting of alternative modes of cooperation on contentious issues that had previously divided the two parties along ethnic lines. Consequently, while KADU joined KANU, resolves and cleavages remained trapped in ethnic interpretations and meanings. The move transferred ethnic strife and competition from regions to Parliament. With increased powers, the presidency became imbued with the patron/client relationships now operating in Parliament. The ethnic rewards and privileges often characteristic of patron/client relations inspired a need to defend the presidency. As the clientele was based on ethnicity, the presidency became jealously guarded along ethnic interest lines and became an object of ethnic defence at all costs. The patron rewarded the clients with jobs in the civil service and other benefits that later had to be undone by the latter president as he installed his own clientele[19].

Furthermore, in both the Kenyatta and the Moi eras, nation building and national unity were framed around ethnic thinking that viewed tribalism as the main threat to national unity. On the other hand, ethnic patronage remained the main lifeline of most political leaders. Paradoxically, ethnicity remained both seduced and rejected by political authorities. In the Moi era, ethnic associations such as the Luo Union, Gikuyu, Embu and Meru Association (GEMA) and the Abaluhya Union were all banned. In the late 1980s and early 1990s as citizens demanded multi-party politics, they were warned of the dangers of a multi-party politics centred on ethnicity. Indeed in the first multi-party elections in 1992 and the second in 1997, ethnic conflicts flared up in a number of provinces.

Yet, even as local politics elicited the trappings of ethnicity, the post-independence period produced local contexts that interacted with new global impulses that were re-framing issues, re-mapping boundaries of coalitions and cleavages, laying the groundwork for broader based thinking on events and national issues and thus, creating new areas of tension motivating alternatives to ethnic based cleavages. As early as the 1970s, cleavages among intellectuals and students marked by student riots at the University of Nairobi brought intellectuals together under Marxist ideologies. On the international arena, 1975 was marked as the beginning of the United Nations Decade for Women that culminated in an international meeting in Nairobi in 1985. This brought new areas of tension and cleavage around gender issues, as women's issues began to rise on the global agenda. The 1980s was a period when Kenyan exiles began organising around attempts to remove Moi from the presidency. Locally, there were increasing tensions among those who were displaced from the only political party, KANU, and left with no alternative avenues or spaces for political expression.

Within these tensions, and particularly in the late 1980s, global and local initiatives and forces were beginning to interact in ways that unveiled diverse and alternative lines of cleavage around issues such as democracy, human rights, gender, justice, freedoms and opposition to authoritarian rule. A post-ethnicity era had clearly surfaced with possible alternative platforms in the formation of new alliances and coalitions and the rise in importance of issues motivating consensus among different groups not necessarily bound to ethnicity, nor framed with ethnicity as the central locus of cleavage. We can argue that such newer lines of cleavage with other bases of motivation point to fragmented ethnicities that are continually being fractured by divided loyalties, increasingly fluid identities, as well as expanding interests and sources of motivations beyond ethnic frames. This happens as more recent alternative lines of cleavages are becoming more readily available to the general populace in the current constitutional review processes that would not have been so obvious in the pre-independence era and the immediate period following independence. The possibility of alternative lines of cleavages allows for experimenting with more diverse compositions of interest groups.

In the 1990s, for example, as civil society questioned human rights abuses associated with a powerful and authoritarian presidency, various groups explored and experimented with newer options of coalition and cleavage for engaging the state; based on common interests and concerns outside the frames of ethnicity. Oginga Odinga and George Anyona, for example, tried to register an opposition socialist party in 1982. There was also an attempt at a coalition around justice issues between the churches and lawyers through the Justice and Peace Convention[20], which was chaired by Bishop Okullu and the Law Society of Kenya (LSK). The Kenya Human Rights Commission was formed as a result of motivations that derived from common interests around human rights. Also, a number of women's organisations such as the League of Kenya Women Voters, the National Committee on the Status of Women, and the Women's Political Caucus were formed along gender lines that made for alternative lines of cleavage. These new coalitions drew from internal forces as much as they were propelled by global impulses, particularly those urging democratisation, and they had clearly shifted away from ethnicity as the motivating force of formation. In the current review process, the interaction between the global and local forces, agents and discourses is reinforced by the increasing use of mobile phones in cities and villages, the availability of internet cafes, free broadcast channels like CNN, Sky News and others, all of which connect Kenyans to almost all parts of the world and vice versa.

This, however, does not mean that ethnicity has been erased, or that there are no further ethnic motivations even within interest groups. Ethnicity remains a powerful force. Party politics in Kenya, in the first multi-party elections in 1992 and again in 1997, suffered tremendously from the entrenched legacy of ethnicity and ethnic trappings in political outlook within the civil society, even as alternative lines of cleavage emerged. The ethnic factor in the split among opposition parties was paramount, and the strong link between party politics and ethnic rivalries and cleavages coloured Kenya's multi party politics in the 1990s almost as extensively as it had coloured the splits and divisions in the constitutional debates around independence.

Yet, in spite of this, the legacy of possible alternative lines of cleavages among the civil society that marked the democratisation process, even as it struggled against ethnicity, point to clear opportunities in the current constitutional review process to move away from ethnic trappings; something not as readily available to the constitution makers in the independence era. Drawing directly from global efforts and local initiatives to have women represented in national decision-making bodies in Kenya via affirmative action, the Constitutional Review Commissioners responded to pressure by Kenyan women to include them as an essential element of the review process (Miguda 2002).

The review itself was also a response to global impulses and local politics that led to demands for greater democratisation and pointed towards the necessity of looking at the constitutional issues that continue to deny rights to Kenyans. Joseph (1997) explains how private Africans and non-African actors steadily increased their efforts on behalf of human rights, civil liberties and pluralist democracy during the 1980s. External forces in particular, narrowed the options available to recalcitrant regimes in ways that weakened their ethnic patronage while at the same time bolstering insurgent groups.

The constitutional review itself is taking place at a time when there is a general critique of Africa and the globalisation process and the impact that globalisation is having on Africa. Amidst all of this are suggestions on possible ways that Africa can manage globalisation, which is seen as inevitable and already present in Africa. There are calls by some African intellectuals regarding the need for Africa to define its place in the new globalising world by fashioning its own modernity (Mazrui 2001). There are fears that globalisation may eclipse Africa, or further marginalize it, making Africa and Africans unequal partners in the global village. This is in contrast to the hope that globalisation will usher Africa into a new phase of development, peace and progress. There are clear calls to counter global power games and define the terms around which Africans can engage globalisation.

Conclusion

There are new cleavages that cut across ethnicity in Kenya's new constitutional debates. Ethnicity has been weakened as a source of cleavage in an era of heightened globalisation. Political tensions and conflicts are now centred, and resolved, around post-ethnicity cleavages, seen particularly in gender and minority group divides. Furthermore, with new global forces taking on currency, there are clear possibilities for these forces to mitigate ethnic differentials and remove the restricted focus on ethnic power and privilege in politics. The civil society that was so vigorous at the height of multi-party debates and democratisation has not settled back into a residual ethnic mould in spite of the occasional slipping in and out of ethnic frames by some current leaders, alternative bases of unity around which to object to political excesses, undemocratic practices and unlawful behaviour by leaders, remain a potential area for crafting forms of democratically oriented cleavages within the civil society that would keep a watchful eye on political proceedings. At the same time, the formation of cleavages counter to the destructive aspects of global forces, or for utilising its more productive possibilities also provide alternative lines of cleavage formation. In the lead up to independence, global and local forces interacted in directions that eclipsed many of these possibilities. The lead up to the comprehensive constitutional review currently taking place has assembled many more alternative lines of interest formation in its wake than was possible in the lead up to the Independence Constitution.

Notes

1. The processes that urged the current constitutional processes ushering in the current constitution began earlier than 2000. However, it is in this year that commissioners were appointed and work on the constitutional review currently in progress began.
2. The first conference in 1960 was to draft the Independence Constitution. The second took place in 1962 to thrash out the differences and disagreements that inevitably arose from global and local issues that the delegates had failed to agree upon in the previous conference. A third conference in 1963 was to finalise constitutional arrangements for independence; the Independence Constitution.
3. These were the four categories of race used by the colonial government in its administrative policies. In addition to these is the category 'other' that appeared in population census. Somalis who did not fit in the four racial categories fell into this group, although they were often also referred to as Somalis.
4. Racial supremacy was encapsulated in the very ideas of a civilizing mission as one of the justifications for colonialism and, in words of key personalities, such as "[t]he white race... is the guardian of values that are essential to the welfare of the black race as well as our own", J. H. Oldham, quoted in Frost (1997: 15).
5. In March, 1944, the Europeans in Kenya formed a new party, the Electors' Union, with the express aim of forging and sustaining white unity in the face of what was seen as the turbulent years ahead. In 1949 they published the Kenya

Plan, which outlined policies spelling out European determination to continue their dominant position in the country. The Kenya Plan advocated a constitution that would give the European community the greatest possible executive control and the maximum amount of local government autonomy outside the native land units (Ogot 2000: 63-64).

6. The Electors' Union for example had a 'Foreign Affairs Department', which liased with representatives in London, and the Joint East and Central African Board. They also developed contacts with influential individuals in Central and Southern Africa, and became a member of United Central Africa Association in Southern Rhodesia.
7. The European electorate had largely united against the colonial government, but was now faced with a growing African nationalism and militarism around Mau Mau. This led to a split in which 6 of the 14 European elected members joined with some Asian elected members to form a non-racial party, the New Kenya Group led by Michael Blundell, while 8 remained on a policy based on the maintenance of their racial superiority, demanding racial segregation and racial supremacy.
8. Wilfred B Havelock remarked that the Europeans had transformed themselves into a small tribe in order to gang up with other smaller tribes against domination and exploitation by larger and more powerful groups, quoted in Munene (2001).
9. For example, there were numerous meetings in the early 1920s among white settlers who resolved to resist, by armed force if necessary, any policy which they believed to involve dangerous concession to Indians. At that time too a deputation of settlers asked for unofficial majority so that among other things, full control would be given them over Indians. See PRO CO 822/4/19, above n 7.
10. See Wilson, PRO CO 822/4/19: the global implications of the local political rivalry between Indians and settlers became clear in the fears expressed by Sir. S. Wilson. He had earlier noted that any alteration of the existing constitution

in Kenya, which would give greater representation to Europeans, and no proportional increase of representation to Indians would reopen the floodgates of the 1923 controversy that would be felt more in India that in Kenya.

11. Somalis had demanded they be classified as Asiatic but this was not granted. The colonial government argued that such a classification would cause an embarrassment to the British Administration in Somaliland and the Northern Frontier Province of Kenya. In the end, Somalis paid non-native poll tax at their own request in order to be distinguished from African natives.
12. Arab witness to the Joint select Committee, Afro-Asian Association petition: Status of Arabs, PRO CO 533/425/20.
13. Both the Lyttelton Constitution of 1954 and the Lennox Boyd Constitution of 1958 (named after the two secretaries of State who proposed them), proposed constitutional changes aimed at providing greater African participation, while maintaining the principle of multiculturalism.
14. In the 1950s, the paradigm of multiculturalism had served as a useful reassurance to the white settlers, imperial power, and Africans. Europeans needed support from Asians, Arabs, and at least some of the Africans in order to maintain white leadership of the country. On the other hand, indigenous black Kenyans saw multi-racialism as an intermediate stage pending black majority rule, see Mazrui (2002: 70).
15. Mazrui (2000: 71) points out that for the Swahili, Asians and Arabs, multiculturalism was a "genuine political lifeline". Ethnic confusions that Swahilised Arabs and Arabised Swahili contributed to the coastal preferences for a multicultural rather than an Afrocentric Kenya.
16. 'Majimbo' was the system of government introduced in Kenya by the Kenya Order in Council legal Notice no. 245 of April 18 1963. It provided for the sharing of executive, legislative and financial powers of the state between central and regional governments (Murungi 1995).
17. The constitutional amendments created a powerful presidency that at the same time weakened the authority of Par-

liament, restricted the arena of political discourse and subordinated holders of constitutional offices to the whim and pleasure of the President (Constitutional Review Commission; 2002: 20-21).

18. It took seven separate amendments, over three years to establish a single-chamber National Assembly, see Ojwang (1990: 115; Ogendo 2001).
19. For example, Adar and Munyae (2001) point out that when Odinga broke away from KANU in 1966 and formed an opposition party, the Kenya People Union (KPU), the Kikuyus began to take an oath to defend the presidency. In the same vein, as Kenyatta's health failed, a group referred to as the 'Kiambu Mafia' tried to change the constitution so that Moi would not automatically take over power from the President. In the Moi era, he resorted to the 'Kalenjinisation' of the Public Service with a concomitant 'de-Kikuyunisation' of the same.
20. The Justice and Peace Convention aimed towards bringing about peaceful changes in Kenya through a public dialogue and increasing peoples understanding of their rights and responsibility as free citizens. See discussion in Friedman (1997).

References

Adar, K., & Munyae, M. (2001) 'Human Rights Abuse in Kenya, under Daniel Arap Moi, 1978 – 2001', *African Studies Quarterly: Online Journal for African Studies*, 5(1): http:/www/web.Africa.ufl.edu/asq/v5/v5ilal.htm, 2001

Barker, C. (1999) *Television, Globalization and Cultural Identities*, Buckingham: Open University Press.

Berman, B. (1998) 'Ethnic Patronage and the Politics of Uncivil Nationalism', *African Affairs*, 99, July.

Cameron, D., PRO CO 822/4/19 Imperial Policy in East Africa, revised memo by Sir Donald Cameron on Federation, 3/6/1927

Chabel, P. (1996) 'The African Crisis: Context and Interpretation', in R. Werbner & T. Ranger (eds), *Postcolonial Identities in Africa*, London: Zed Books.

Constitution of Kenya Review Commission, (2002) 'The People's Choice', *The Main Report of the Constitution of Kenya Review Commission*, Nairobi, 18th September: http://www.kenyaconstitution.org/docs/03d005.htm

Featherstone, M. (1995) *Undoing Culture: Globalization, Postmodernism and Identity*, London: SAGE Publications.

Fraser, H., The Kenya Constitutional Question: A Note. PRO CO 822/599.

Friedman G. (1997) 'Church and State in Kenya, 1986 – 1992: The Church's Involvement in the 'Game of Change'', *African Affairs*, 96(382), pp. 25-52.

Frost, R. (1997), *Race Against Time: Human Relations and Politics in Kenya Before Independence*, Transafrica Press.

Joseph, R. (1997) 'Democratisation in Africa after 1989: Comparative and Theoretical Perspectives', *Comparative Politics*, 29(3), pp. 363-382.

Leys, C. (1975), *Underdevelopment in Kenya; The Political Economy of Neocolonialism 1964-1971*, University of California Press.

Maxon, R. (2000) 'The Colonial and Foreign Offices: Policy & Control', in B. Ogot, & W. Ochieng (eds.), *Kenya, The Making of a Nation: A Hundred Years of Kenya's History, 1895-1995*, Institute of Research & Postgraduate Studies, Maseno University.

Mazrui, A. (2000) 'Arab and Swahili Dreams & Fears, 1939-1963', in B. Ogot, & W. Ochieng (eds), *Kenya, The Making of a Nation: A Hundred Years of Kenya's History, 1895-1995*, Institute of Research & Postgraduate Studies, Maseno University.

Miguda, E. (2002) 'Engendering Democracy in Kenya: Effects of Multi-Party Electoral System on Women Participation in Politics', in L. Chweya (ed), *Electoral Politics in Kenya*, Nairobi: Claripress.

Munene, M. (2001) *The Manipulation of the Constitution of Kenya: 1963 – 1996, A Reflective Essay. In* The Constitution: Past, Present and Amendments, Constitution of Kenya Review Commission (CKRC), http://www.kenyaconstitution.org/docs/03d008.htm

Murungi Kiraitu (1995) 'Ethnicity & Multi-partism in Kenya', *Thoughts on Democracy Series,* 3.

Odhiambo-Atieno, E.S, *'Mugo's Prophesy' in* Ogot, B. (2002) 'The Settler Dream for a White Dominion', in B. Ogot, & W. Ochieng (eds), *Kenya, The making of a Nation: A Hundred Years of Kenya's History, 1895-1995*, Institute of Research & Postgraduate Studies, Maseno University.

Odinga, O. (1967), *Not Yet Uhuru: The Autobiography of Oginga Odinga*, London: Heinemann.

Ogendo, O. (2001) *The Politics of Constitutional Change in Kenya since Independence,*

1963 – 1969. in, The Constitution: Past, Present and Amendments, Constitution of Kenya Review Commission (CKRC), http://www.kenyaconstitution. org/docs/03d008.htm

Ojwang, J. (1990), *Constitutional Development in Kenya: Institutional Adaptation and Social Change*, Nairobi: Acts Press.

Ogot, B. (2002) 'The Settler Dream for a White Dominion', in B. Ogot, & W. Ochieng (eds), *Kenya, The Making of a Nation: A Hundred Years of Kenya's History, 1895-1995*, Institute of Research & Postgraduate Studies, Maseno University.

Chapter 7

Economic Partnership Agreements: Reducing Poverty Through Enhancing Regional Integration Between the ACP and the EU

Teresa Thorp

The Cotonou Agreement, the Partnership Agreement between the Members of the African, Caribbean and Pacific (ACP) Group of States on one side, and the European Community (EU) and its Member States on the other, was signed on 23 June 2000 and affirms two central objectives: to eradicate poverty and to enhance global integration[1]. Both objectives pose a significant challenge for the member states. The majority of ACP countries are poor and vulnerable, 40 are least developed countries (LDC's)[2]; and despite persistent efforts, they are yet to integrate into the world economy.

This is evidenced in the ACP share in world exports, which fell from 3.4 % in 1976 to 1.9 % in 2000 and their share in developing countries' exports, which fell from 13.3 % in 1976 to 3.7 % in 2000. The evolution of trade with the EU has followed a similar pattern. The share of EU imports from the ACP in total EU imports decreased, falling from 6.7% in 1976 to 2.8% in 2000, and the share of imports from the ACP in total imports from developing countries (excluding countries in transition) fell from 14.8 % in 1976 to 6% in 2000 (ECDGT/DGD 2002:2; Bilateral Trade Relations ACP). As a consequence, success has been disparate. Although EU trade with the ACP countries totalled over 58 billion Euro Dollars in 2001, there has been a heavy weighting towards the more developed African economies (Bilateral Trade Relations ACP). Nigeria (21% of ACP exports), Ivory Coast (7%), Angola (6%) and Cameroon (6%) are the EU's most important exporters. Diversification of trade is rare and 'cream-skimming' of raw materials remains rife. In 2001, 10 products accounted for 60 % of total ACP exports to the Community. Petroleum oil was the most important ACP export (29% of total ACP exports or 9.25 billion Euro Dollars). Exports in diamonds (10%), cocoa (4%), wood (4%), sugar (3%), aluminium (2%), coffee (2%), tobacco (2%), and bananas (2%) followed. Raw materials represented the bulk of all exports with finished goods making up 21% of ACP exports to the EU.

All in all the results have not lived up to expectations: "trade preferences have not prevented the ACP from being increasingly marginalized in world trade, they have not prevented the continued decrease in the ACP's share in total EU imports nor have they overcome the high dependence of the ACP on a few commodities" (ECDGT/DGD 2002: 2). The ebb and flow of multilateralism and universalism of trade has mostly meant that the poorest ACP countries continue to be marginalized, enduring only as spectators to the global stage. This backdrop leads one to ask whether the Economic Partnership Agreement's (EPA's) will be successful where preceding negotiations and Conventions, principally economic structural reforms, have failed to integrate the ACP states into the global economy.

Closer economic relationships between the African, Caribbean and Pacific States and the European Union have evolved over a fifty-year period. They were incorporated into the Treaty of Rome in 1957 (Article 131), and cemented by a series of other conventions: Yaounde I & II (1963 and 1969 respectively), and the Lomé Conventions (1975-1995). The conventions enlarged the ACP pact and focused on progressive market liberalization initiatives. Today, 79 ACP countries are signatories to the ACP-EU Partnership Agreement. Yet, the majority continue to linger on the fringe of global trade.

Earlier efforts indicate that an appreciation of the regional implications for the ACP-EU Economic Partnership Agreement's is imperative. One feature of these implications revolves around whether global economic integration is best put forward from an 'inter-regional' or an 'intra-regional' basis. This paper opens the debate on such issues, first by exploring the nature of the EPA's from an inter-regional perspective and then by highlighting the challenges of managing the plethora of intra-regional agreements. More precisely, what are the regional implications for the Economic Partnership Agreements, and can they be used as a catalyst for sustained change?

As a starting point, four important dimensions emerge from the regional trade liberalization roadmap. First, the EPA's are partnership agreements. They imply rights and obligations for both sides. Second, negotiation rounds must fit within relevant WTO rules. Negotiations must be attuned to multilateral trade developments. Third, the EPA's must consider the development and the socio-economic impact of trade measures on ACP countries. This includes an assessment of special treatment for least-developed ACP countries, which would include duty-free and quota-free treatment for their exports. Fourth, alternative arrangements need to be established where EPA's are not possible. This paper explores such regional implications for the ACP-EU Economic Partnership Agreements and extracts a number of concerns.

COTONOU IN PERSPECTIVE

In practice, the EPA's adopt a two-pronged policy approach: trade liberalization between the ACP and the EU, or *inter-regional integration;* and trade liberalization within the ACP regional grouping, or *intra-regional integration.* In doing so, the EPA's aim to "establish the timetable for the progressive removal of barriers to trade between the Parties, in accordance with the relevant WTO rules" (Cotonou Agreement 2000: Article 37.7).

EPA dialogue officially started on the 27th September 2002 and the negotiations are to be concluded by 31 December 2007. The regional EPA's will therefore be set in place from 1 January 2008[3]. In the interim period, non-reciprocal Lomé IV trade preferences will continue to apply (2000-2007). This will meet with the WTO waiver for LDC's[4]. Within the preceding context, the five-year timeline for EPA negotiations may seem ambitious. Concerns over the slow progress in achieving the objectives of the Phase I EPA negotiations, which includes concluding on principles and objectives as well as issues of common interest to the entire group, have already emerged. Accordingly, the ACP Council of Ministers has planned a special review session before the end of September 2003 and in preparation for the 2nd ACP-EU Ministerial Meeting on the EPA Negotiation round (GSACP 2003). Similarly, the EU recognizes the importance of the regional trade liberalization roadmap:

> in preparing for EPA's, we will put a strong accent on the strengthening and deepening of regional economic integration within the different ACP sub-regions. The current situation of

> market fragmentation often discourages investment and hinders trade. The aim of EPA's will be to create larger, more attractive markets for local and foreign investors (ECDGT/DGD 2002: 1).

To support these partnership obligations, the EU has assigned significant financial aid to the process. The 9th European Development Fund covers up to 13.5 billion Euro Dollars, and examples of EU assistance for ACP trade policy include: 10 and 20 million Euro Dollars for ACP, WTO and EPA support programmes; 1.4 million Euro Dollars in support for ACP countries to be present in Geneva where WTO activities take place; and a 50 million Euro Dollar facility for the integration of ACP countries into the global economy (ECDGT/DGD 2002: 9). In the course of the recent programming of funds for the next 5 years, 350 million Euro Dollars has been earmarked for regional integration and trade related technical assistance and capacity building (ECDGT/DGD 2002: 11).

Even so, a number of tactical questions remain unanswered. To work, the dynamics of this policy framework must reflect not only traditional thinking on market access, but must adopt potential growth strategies that will facilitate the effective integration of the ACP Member States into the global economy. How exactly will the transition proceed? What is the appropriate mix of *inter-regional* and *intra-regional* agreements? What are the political, economic, cultural and social aspects of managing change and how does one reduce the associated negative externalities? How will the potential for derogations ensure that fragmentation between the ACP states and the EU does not increase?[5] In the absence of a more defined program of change, the answers to these questions remain nebulous. It necessitates appraisal within the institutional framework of the WTO, the EU and the ACP, and from both *inter-regional* and *intra-regional* trade perspectives.

THE COMPLEXITY OF INTER-REGIONAL TRADE: FITTING THE EPA'S TO THE WTO RULES

The fundamental aim of the EPA's is to fit within the relevant WTO rules (Onguglo & Ito 2003). In this sense, the Cotonou Agreement and the principal WTO Accords are compatible in terms of aiming to eradicate poverty and integrate the ACP member states into the global economy, by adopting a series of initiatives that will pave the way to trade liberalization (i.e. removal of barriers to trade, improvement of market access, partnerships in goods and services, and the protection and promotion of investment). In principle, these initiatives are universal. They hinge on the two cornerstones of WTO trade law: non-discrimination and reciprocity.

'National treatment', the first pillar to the multilateral trading system, condemns discrimination between foreign and national goods or services and service suppliers or between foreign and national holders of intellectual property rights. (Article III of the 1994 GATT for Trade in Goods; Article XVII of GATS in Relation to Trade in Services; and Article 3 of TRIPS with Respect to the Protection of Intellectual Property). Whereas the second pillar, the 'Most-Favoured-Nation' clause (MFN), assures that "all nations are equal and treated equally" (Article I of 1994 GATT; Article II GATS; and Article 4 TRIPs).

Nonetheless, these rules are not supreme. Certain derogations are acknowledged, mainly to ensure equitable participation in global trade. To do otherwise, would mean that the majority of developing countries would be inflicted with disproportionate adjustment costs. This would hold true for a large number of ACP member states. To some extent, however, the derogations are controversial. Added to this is that they are integrated within a complex mesh of legal texts, of which a few examples are provided here.

Interpretation of Article XXIV (World Trade Organisation) of the 1994 GATT on 'Regional Trade Agreements', and the Uruguay Understanding on that Article (Uruguay Round Agreement), is but one case in point. One may argue that Article XXIV does not contain adequate Special and Differential Treatment (SDT) for developing countries. In fact, it is silent on the specific nature of such provisions. However, this is not to say that such provisions are entirely absent from the WTO Accords. The need for additional flexibility in GATT obligations for the developing countries, albeit limited, was first recognized at the 1954-1955 Review Session. Article XVIII was revised to recognise the structural nature of the balance-of-payments problem in developing countries (Michalopoulos 2000: 4)[10]. It was here that the concept of Special and Differential Treatment was introduced.

The 1979 revision of Part IV of the GATT on 'Trade and Development', now known as the 'Enabling Clause', consolidated the concept of 'differential and more favourable treatment' enabling members to derogate from the MFN Clause. It stipulates that "notwithstanding the provisions of Article I of the General Agreement, contracting parties may accord differential and more favourable treatment to developing countries, without according such treatment to other contracting parties". In other words, developed contracting parties may accord preferential tariff treatment to products originating in developing countries in accordance with the Generalized System of Preferences.

While the 'Enabling Clause' formally embodied the concept of special and differential treatment, it continued to do so discretionally, rather than in legally binding terms. The 1994 Uruguay interpretation on these derogations kept matters murky; the specific needs of the LDCs were to stay "under review"[7]. Future drafting did little to clear the haze. Part IV of the 1994 GATT on Trade and Development is emblematical. Article XXXVI mooted the principle of non-reciprocity again but still allowed for broad interpretation. (See: http://www.wto.org/english/docs_e/legal_e/gatt47_02_e.htm). As a result, definitional and contextual arguments have arisen. To illustrate, Article XXXVI.8 provides that "the developed contracting parties do not expect reciprocity for commitments made by them in trade negotiations to reduce or remove tariffs and other barriers to the trade of less-developed contracting parties". It is argued that the intended context of Article XXXVI.8 is multilateral and not regional.

On the contrary, where services are concerned, economic integration in GATS Article V:3(a) explicitly provides flexibility for developing countries to meet conditions regarding substantial sectoral coverage and with respect to eliminating discriminatory measures in accordance with the level of development. In addition, Article V:3(b) explicitly distinguishes between Regional Trade Agreements. It differentiates between developed and developing countries by providing treatment that is more favourable to LDC's. (See: http://www.wto.org/english/docs_e/legal_e/26-gats_01_e.htm). In view of this, fitting the EPA's to WTO laws remains open to interpretation. In order to presuppose compatibility, regional integration accords have often gone beyond the WTO provisions.

The Cotonou Agreement provides for the consideration of the development and socio-economic impacts of trade measures on the ACP countries, and their capacity to adapt and adjust their economies to the liberalization process. For instance, Part 5 of the Agreement provides for special treatment for the least developed, landlocked and island ACP states (LDLICS). Article 84.1. (Chapter 1) stipulates that,

> to enable LDLICS to take full advantage of the opportunities offered by the Agreement so as to step up their respective rates of development, cooperation shall ensure special treatment for the least developed ACP countries and take due account of the vulnerability of landlocked and island ACP countries. It shall also take into consideration the needs of countries in post-conflict situations.

Article 85.1. (Chapter 2, 'Least Developed ACP States') goes even further: "the least-developed ACP States shall be accorded a special treatment in order to enable them to overcome the serious economic and social difficulties hindering their development so as to step up their respective rates of development".

By the same token, the EU has acknowledged the importance of SDT. As referenced by EU Trade Commissioner, Pascal Lamy (2003), at the 6th Meeting of African, Caribbean and Pacific (ACP) Trade Ministers: "Both the EU and ACP countries consider the development dimension as the key element of the Doha Agenda. Whether on agriculture, on industrial tariffs, or on access to medicines we must ensure that we respond to the concerns and expectations of developing countries". Again, the statement is political; left open to interpretation.

Admittedly, some advances have been made on the DDA front. Both parties agreed to:

- Work together to ensure that the DDA maintains a fair and important level of preferences for industrial and agricultural products for ACP countries and that trade opening takes place in a gradual and flexible manner;

- Call for an urgent solution to the issue of access to medicines for countries with no manufacturing capacity in accordance with the Doha mandate;
- Work together to establish rules giving developing countries special and differential treatment to help them better integrate into the world trading system;
- Support accession to the WTO of Least Developed Countries, most of which are ACP countries;
- Underline the importance of trade related assistance and capacity building measures to allow developing countries to better benefit from international trade (see The Doha Declaration explained, http://www.wto.org/english/tratop_e/dda_e/dohaexplained_e.htm#ldc).

An intent to impart derogations to the developing countries is clear. Derogations are provided for both within the WTO legal texts and within the Cotonou Agreement itself. Even so, there exists an important legal lacuna with respect to WTO trade law and the integration of special and differentiated treatment in the EPA's. Article XXIV of the 1994 GATT on 'Regional Trade Agreements' that would apply to EPA's between developed and developing countries is silent on SDT; and Part IV on 'Trade and Development' has been mostly applied to intra-regional agreements (i.e. agreements between developing countries). These issues may be addressed collectively via the Doha Development Agenda, either through the reform of Article XXIV or through the reform of Part IV. For all intents and purposes, the WTO needs to consider both platforms to ensure harmony between 'Regional Agreements' and 'Trade and Development'.

The 2003 5th WTO Ministerial meeting in Cancun (Mexico) (World Trade Organisation 2003) will provide a unique juncture for the ACP Group of States to actively engage in ensuring that the EPA's are compatible with WTO rules (PACPTMM 2003)[8]. Special and differentiated treatment for least-developed ACP countries may result in heated debate, but this is healthy. At the same time, the ACP pact should table specific trade related issues for developing countries including the nature of competition policy and subsidies, particularly with relation to petroleum exports and agriculture. Concerted practices, the abuse of dominant positions and 'cream-skimming' can critically challenge the productivity and efficiency gains potentially generated by trade liberalization.

Conversely, Cancun will stumble if the developed countries are unwilling to negotiate on STD [Such a failure did indeed occur. Eds note.]. For them, such failure will be under the guise of setbacks on specific issues, such as agriculture and the four principle Singapore issues: (i) trade and foreign investment, (ii) trade and competition, (iii) transparency in government procurement and (iv) trade facilitation, were raised by the developed economies during the Singapore Ministerial Conference of the WTO in 1996. These issues are important but to advance global trade negotiations they need to be set within the overall framework of STD and Regional Trade Agreements.

Unmistakably, the liberalisation of agriculture at a regional level, which constitutes 37% of ACP exports to the EU (EU-ACP Bilateral Trade Relations), should be given a high priority in any EPA. Consequently, the effects of the Common Agriculture Policy on ACP structural reforms are significant. The WTO forum may well deal with such issues, but they too remain sensitive, especially if not considered within the overall context of STD and regionalisation.

The issue of sanitary and phytosanitary standards, and the technical and financial difficulties faced by the ACP countries in meeting these standards, is also a critical link to the liberalization of agricultural trade. Divergent marketing rules or product regulations (e.g. standards, sanitary, veterinary or phytosanitary rules, rules for the protection of the environment or the protection of consumers) and costly compliance requirements can act as practical barriers to trade or result in high cost and inefficiencies (ECDGT/DGD 2002: 6). Barring the ACP countries from trade on standards issues needs to be raised within regional integration, trade and development and competition forums.

The EU may argue that they have committed to supporting the ACP members in efforts to meet standards in certain domains. For example, "[t]he EU earmarked 29 million Euro Dollars for horticultural assistance in July 2001 and 42.7 million Euro Dollars for the fishery program in December 2002" (EU-ACP Bilateral Trade Relations). Nonetheless, the benchmarks for success still need to tie in poverty and global integration. After all, these are the umbrella objectives. The same issues are equally true for the liberalization of trade in services, which is acknowledged in the WTO Accords and the Cotonou Agreement. Article 41.4 of the Cotonou Agreement stipulates that: "the Parties further agree on the objective of extending under the economic partnership agreements ... to encompass the liberalization of services". This will include the substantial domains of tourism and restructuring within the banking and insurance sectors.

Furthermore, liberalization of capital remains as important, if not more so, as liberalization in goods and services and will have diverse implications for inter-regional integration and the EPA negotiation rounds. Global integration demands a greater availability of credit, which goes hand in hand with access for, and protection of, the private sector. Article 78.3 of the Cotonou Agreement, 'Investment Protection', stipulates that: "The Parties also agree to introduce, within the economic partnership agreements ... general principles on protection and promotion of investments, which will endorse the best results agreed in the competent international fora or bilaterally". Likewise, the EPA's will need to ensure adequate protection of intellectual capital and property rights. Be that as it may, freeing up factors of production and adopting a competitive framework are not enough to eradicate poverty and to integrate the ACPs into the global economy. An increased focus needs to be placed on the complementary implications of intra-regional ACP trade.

Intra-regional Trade and Regional Institutional Reform

Conventionally, intra-regional integration may be thought of with respect to four main models: free trade zones, customs unions, an EU type common market model (with its four freedoms of goods, services, people and capital), and that of an economic and monetary union. Within this framework, the ACP countries are always one step behind the more developed nations. As a consequence, whether the EU model of regional integration is appropriate for the ACP countries is questionable. This is not to say that advances in EU integration cannot provide useful insights into advancing ACP intra-regional integration. The European Commission has gone some way in setting out 'Orientations on the Qualification of ACP Regions for the Negotiation of EPA's' (EPA Watch). However, the structures and sequencing of intra-regionalisation may be different, and will certainly depend upon unique political and cultural factors within the ACP regions. Fundamentally, intra-regional trade demands ACP countries to integrate deeply and to establish good governance, and these issues need to be linked directly to the EPA negotiations.

Harmonizing certain trade policies may proceed more quickly at an intra-regional level. Provisions already stipulated in the Cotonou Agreement include Competition Policy (Article 45), Protection of Intellectual Property Rights (Article 46), Standardization and Certification (Article 47), Sanitary and Phytosanitary Measures (Article 48), Trade and Environment (Article 49), Trade and Labour Standards (Article 50) and Consumer Policy and Protection of Consumer Health (Article 51). Furthermore, enforcement mechanisms are integrated within the strategies on economic and trade cooperation (Part 3). Whether in the form of the European Court of Justice, or through binding arbitration, integration initiatives within the ACP region must be supported by credible enforcement mechanisms. This will aid global alignment.

'Priority setting' is another intra-regional implication with respect to the trade liberalization roadmap. On the one hand, the EU is concentrated on its expansion program: 10 new countries will join the EU in 2004. Admittedly, this will open a broader market to the ACP countries. However, there is little indication that the EU will have the resources available to assist the ACP countries with their own agendas for intra-regional integration. On the other hand, harmonization with the ACP countries is particularly complex. Market structures are completely different. Efficient competitive markets are the exception rather than the rule, capacity building in the ACP regions is in its infancy, and a large and heterogeneous private sector will be unable to bear the consequences of liberal reform, such as privatisation, and the resulting retrenchment in education and jobs.

All these factors raise the questions of whether inter-regional trade liberalization will be unshielded leaving the LDCs exposed to powerful industrial economies and a well-established trading pact. The implications for the ACP countries are considerable. Not opening the ACP countries to trade may have adverse effects with the possibility of the EU withdrawing from financial aid and trade related technical assistance. First, without aid it is questionable as to whether trade diversification can really occur. Secondly, the ACP countries are all highly dependent on technology transfer from developed regions, notably from the EU, but also from the US. Accordingly, intra-regional market integration is important for the attraction of foreign direct investment (FDI).

Intra-regional implications are thus as equally important as inter-regional implications, and it is within this context that intra-regional bodies have to be the motor for change. Will there be time for this transition, or will the ACP countries remain marginalized resulting in an ongoing fragmentation of global trade? The answer to this question will be driven by the Doha Round and the decision-making processes at the heart of the WTO. Added to this are two further questions. First, will the DDA promote differentiated levels of trade liberalization? Second, will the WTO support intra-regional market development? These are the supplementary questions that the 79 strong ACP block will need to position on the policy agenda at Cancun.

Within the superfluity of intra-regional accords, a number of intra-regional implications may be highlighted. Three concrete examples follow: the New Partnership for Africa's Development (NEPAD) in Africa, the Caribbean Community Secretariat (CARICOM), and the PICTA/PACER Accords in the Pacific (Pacific Islands Secretariat). Regional integration in Africa has been gradual (Iqbal & Khan 1998). The West African Economic and Monetary Union

(WAEMU) made progress with the entry into effect of the Customs Union in 2000. The Central African Economic and Monetary Community (CEMAC) has focused on establishing a single market. The NEPAD, however, is an African owned initiative based on a common vision and shared conviction to reduce poverty, to accelerate growth and to end increasing marginalisation on the continent (Funke & Nsouli 2003). It encourages participation in the Doha Development Agenda (DDA) and conforms to WTO Accords. Implementation details are still sketchy but the aim is to promote regional integration as an engine of economic growth and development. Emphasis is on trade and market access, dismantling non-tariff barriers and export diversification, which, taken as a whole, should strengthen both inter-regional trade and intra-African trade.

To promote growth, the NEPAD's action plan focuses on three key priorities. First is capacity building for trade policy, market access strategies, trade negotiations skills and related institutional development. Second is regulatory compliance and strengthening the institutional and administrative framework. Third is overcoming supply-side impediments, like market diversification (in such areas as sustainable tourism and professional services) and in meeting relevant environmental and sanitary and phytosanitary standards.

Another priority for the NEPAD will be increasing transparency through the integration of the informal sector (Thorp 2003). This sector constitutes between 20% and 37% of the total GDP in Benin, Burkina Faso, Chad, Mali, Mauritania, Niger, Senegal and Tunisia (Charmes 1998). To exacerbate the problem "at least 65 percent of Africa's working population works without legislation, insurance, employee protection or rules" (Kindenberg 2002); and the sector is growing. In Zambia, the informal sector is growing faster than the formal sector in terms of business (The

Times of Zambia 2003). In Zimbabwe, the informal sector is the country's biggest employer (Kumbawa 2002).

These issues are complex, and they will influence EPA negotiations. The voice of the private sector will need to be harnessed not only for equitable participation in the global multilateral trading system but to influence the EPA negotiating rounds. The rationale is to ensure that the private sector is able to capitalize on opportunities from liberalized markets.

Likewise, in the Caribbean, fostering trust in intra-regional institutions such as the Caribbean Community (CARICOM) is difficult. Many members continue to act in their own self-interest. In 2002, Jamaica went outside of CARICOMs collective negotiations to sign an air services agreement with the US Federal Aviation Administration (US Dept. of Transportation 2002). For the Bahamas, with its lower unemployment rate and higher per capita GDP, the problem is one of unregulated migration (Ingraham 2001). Implementing a proposed regional free trade zone allowing for the free movement of labour and capital, common external tariffs and a single monetary standard is challenging; and the Caribbean Single Market Economy (CSME) will have to evolve over time. This is where enforcement mechanisms and institutional and administrative reform are necessary. Unfettered financial markets in the Caribbean deter legitimate enterprise development and impede intra-regional integration. Some of these issues could be addressed by the WTO from a demand-side perspective.

Governance in the South Pacific poses similar issues, though the context is slightly different. The aim remains one of reducing poverty and integrating LDCs within the global economy. For the most part, the Pacific Island countries are in a state of transition moving from subsistence to industrial economies. They are open to manipulation due to their relatively fragile economic position and the curbing of financial loopholes in Europe and the Caribbean. Until recently, offshore financial centre income has been a major source of foreign exchange revenue for many (Seneviratne 2000), which otherwise have little or no resources to export (Ellison 2002). Again, transparency and the eradication of money laundering and corruption provide the base to improved governance, whilst regional unification is essential to development and integration in the global arena. Sanctions are not the answer.

In the Pacific, delicate issues persist. Increased intra-regional trading with the more wealthy Pacific states of Australia and New Zealand, and the implications of integrating the French Territories, such as New Caledonia, French Polynesia and Wallis and Fatuna, into intra-regional trading accords must be explored. Failure to do this will mean that the least developed countries will continue to act on an unlevel playing field. They will continue to be exploited by offshore cartels, and non-competitive market liberalization will ruin havoc on their economies. Curbing trans-national crime and improving economic integration need to be encouraged from within the regions, and trade needs to focus on increasing economic social welfare.

Both the Pacific Agreement on Closer Economic Relations (PACER) and the Pacific Island Countries Trade Agreement (PICTA) have gone some way towards addressing these issues (Pacific Islands Secretariat). PACER establishes a framework agreement setting out the basis for the future development of trade relations among all 16 Pacific Forum members. At the same time, PICTA is a free trade Agreement among the Pacific Forum Island Countries. It will be introduced gradually, over the next 10 years, and lead to the establishment of a free trade area. It is within these Accords that the Pacific acknowledges the indispensability of intra-regional integration.

Conclusion

Are Economic Partnership Agreements in themselves sufficient to sustain growth and eradicate poverty? Or, is there a need for deeper *intra-regional* integration within a political and cultural policy framework? It is doubtful whether, in the absence of such integration, the economic welfare of the ACP countries can improve greatly. Handpicking of the leading economies, such as Nigeria, the Ivory Coast, Angola and Cameroon, will continue; and it is within this context that a potential fragmentation of the Cotonou Agreement will occur. Intra-regional institutional reform is an essential stepping-stone to trade liberalization in this context.

One needs to reconsider the premise that all are created equal and can trade equally. Leveraging the EU's commitment to reform is therefore an issue for the joint ACP-EC Ministerial Trade Committee. If the WTO is to play an active part in eradicating poverty and integrating the LDC's into the global economy then it too will need to play a stronger role in the establishment of intra-regional accords. The direction for the ACP countries will be to table their requirements for special and differentiated treatment within the WTO forum. Any attempt to establish a new institutional mechanism for global trade negotiation will be a lengthy process, resulting in long delays and little result. In this light, the capacity of the ACP group to engage in collective bargaining will be its strongpoint. However in order to traverse the global political quagmire, collective bargaining will need to be leveraged through intra-regional institutional reform.

The Cotonou Agreement provides a defined window of opportunity for the ACP region to leverage into the global economy through the future Economic Partnership Agreements. As such, one of the major tests will be the proclivity of the Cotonou Agreement to act as a catalyst in forming intra-regional alliances as one step towards global integration. If done in isolation, these arrangements will result in more of the same; that is, continued fragmentation. Alternatively, a co-ordinated and dynamic roadmap should lead to success on three fronts: intra-regional trade, inter-regional trade, and global integration.

Nonetheless, the question rests as to how to proceed in co-ordinating Regional Trade Agreements. As illustrated creating this dynamic roadmap is one of the biggest challenges facing the global policy-making community. One could argue that the WTO is perhaps best positioned to harmonize Regional Trade Agreements at a global level. Its juxtaposed role would be to act as the coordinator of this complex global trade web and in turn aid in ensuring the successful implementation of the Economic Partnership Agreements. In this sense, the ACP partner countries will not be impeded on their path to development, marginalisation and fragmentation of global trade will eventually be reduced, and regional integration will serve as a catalyst to eradicating poverty and to enhancing global integration.

Notes

1 General Secretariat of the African, Caribbean and Pacific Group of States, http://www.acpsec.org; Directorate-General European Commission,'Trade & Development': http://europa.eu.int/comm/trade, & development; on EU-ACP bilateral Trade relations, see: http://europa.eu.int/comm/trade/bilateral/acp/acp.htm; 'The Cotonou Agreement', Article 1: Objectives of the Partnership.

2 Forty-nine countries are currently designated by the United Nations as 'least developed countries' (LDCs). The list is reviewed every 3 years by the Economic and Social Council (ECOSOC). The criteria underlying the current list of LDCs are: (a) low income, as measured by the gross domestic product (GDP) per capita; (b) weak human resources, as mea-

sured by a composite index (Augmented Physical Quality of Life Index) based on indicators of life expectancy at birth, per capita calorie intake, combined primary and secondary school enrolment, and adult literacy; (c) a low level of economic diversification, as measured by a composite index (Economic Diversification Index) based on the share of manufacturing in GDP, the share of the labour force in industry, annual per capita commercial energy consumption, and UNCTAD's merchandise export concentration index. "There are currently 49 countries considered to be the least developed countries (LDCs), 39 of which are ACP countries ... This category of countries is distinguished by the level of poverty of the population and the lack of economic, institutional and human resources", http://europa.eu.int/scadplus/leg/en/lvb/r12400.htm. "Of the 79 ACP states, 40 are considered to be least developed countries (LDC)", Bianchi, S. *German and EU Development Policy, Poor Countries Concerned over EU Enlargement*, http://www.ips-cic-kommunikationsprojekt.net/d_eu_ewipol/uk/artikel_104.html.

3 "In order to facilitate the transition to the new trading arrangements, the non-reciprocal trade preferences applied under the Fourth ACP-EC Convention shall be maintained during the preparatory period for all ACP countries, under the conditions defined in Annex V", 'The Cotonou Agreement': Article 36.3, 'Modalities'. "EPA's shall be negotiated during the preparatory period which shall end by 31 December 2007 at the latest. Formal negotiations of the new trading arrangements shall start in September 2002 and the new trading arrangements shall enter into force by 1 January 2008, unless earlier dates are agreed between the Parties", Article 37.1 Procedures.

4 Marrakech Agreement, *Preferential Tariff treatment for Least-Developed Countries, Decision on Waiver*, Adopted on 15 June 1999(1), "Members, acting pursuant to the provisions of paragraph 3 of Article IX of the WTO Agreement, Decide that: 1. Subject to the terms and conditions set out hereunder, the provisions of paragraph 1 of Article

I of the GATT 1994 shall be waived until 30 June 2009, to the extent necessary to allow developing country Members to provide preferential tariff treatment to products.of least-developed countries, designated as such by the United Nations, without being required to extend the same tariff rates to like products of any other Member". http://www.wto.org/english/docs_e/legal_e/waiver1999_e.htm.

5 In 2004, "the Community will assess the situation of the non-LDC which, after consultations with the Community decide that they are not in a position to enter into economic partnership agreements and will examine all alternative possibilities, in order to provide these countries with a new framework for trade which is equivalent to their existing situation and in conformity with WTO rules", 'The Cotonou Agreement': Article 37.6, 'Procedures'.

6 Three main provisions were agreed, 2 of them relating to Article XVIII. Article XVIII (B) were revised to include a specific provision to allow countries at 'an early stage of their development' to adopt quantitative restrictions on imports whenever monetary reserves were deemed to be inadequate in terms of the country's long term development strategy. Article XVIII (C) was revised to allow for the imposition of trade restrictions (both tariffs and quantitative restrictions) to support infant industries with a view to raising living standards. And a provision granting the right of veto to certain effected contracting parties was deleted, thus making the imposition of quantitative restrictions easier (Michalopoulos 1998:4).

7 Uruguay Round, Ministerial Decisions adopted by the Trade Negotiations Committee on 15 December 1993 and 14 April 1994, 'Measures in favour of least-developed countries'. "Reaffirming their commitment to implement fully the provisions concerning the least-developed countries contained in paragraphs 2(d), 6 and 8 of the Decision of 28 November 1979 on Differential and More Favourable Treatment, Reciprocity and Fuller Participation of Developing Countries; 3. Agree to keep under review the specific needs of the least-developed countries and to continue to seek the

adoption of positive measures which facilitate the expansion of trading opportunities in favour of these countries", see: http://www.wto.org/english/docs_e/legal_e/31-dlldc_e.htm#31.

8 "Pacific ACP Trade Ministers met in Nadi, Fiji, on 4 July 2003 to discuss the current state of negotiations between the African, Caribbean and Pacific (ACP) Group and the European Union (EU) on Economic Partnership Agreements (EPA's) under the Cotonou Agreement and the preparations for future regional EPA negotiations. The Ministers also agreed on Forum Island Country (FIC) positions in preparation for the World Trade Organisation (WTO) Ministerial Conference to take place in Cancun in September 2003" (PACPTMM 2003).

References

Bilateral Trade Relations; Africa, Caribbean, Pacific, http://europa.eu.int/comm/trade/issues/bilateral/regions/acp/index_en.htm

Caribbean Community (CARICOM) Secretariat http://www.caricom.org/

CEMAC, Communauté Économique et Monétaire de l'Afrique Centrale, http://www.cemac.org.

Charmes, J. (1998) *Women Working in the Informal Sector in Africa; New Methods and New Data,* paper presented to the United Nations Statistics Division; the Gender and Development Programme of the United Nations Development Programme (UNDP); & the project "Women in Informal Employment: Globalizing and Organizing" (WIEGO) http://www.wiego.org/papers/3informal.html

Ellison, C. (2002) Opening Address of the Asia/Pacific Group on Money Laundering, Fifth Annual Meeting, Brisbane, 5 June 2002, http://www.ag.gov.au/www/justice ministerHome.nsf/0/C1A7F0F4094851C9CA256BD0000B503E?OpenDocument

EPA Watch: http://www.epawatch.net/general/enupage.php?menuID=5.

European Commission Directorate-General for Trade/Directorate-General for Development (2002) *Economic Partnership Agreements, Start of Negotiations - A New Approach in the Relations Between the European Union and the ACP Countries*, Belgium: European Communities.

EU-ACP bilateral Trade relations, http://europa.eu.int/comm/trade/bilateral/acp/acp.htm.

Funke, N. & Nsouli, S. (2003) 'New Partnership for Africa's Development: Opportunities and Challenges', *IMF Working Paper,* IMF Institute WP/03/69.

General Secretariat of the African, Caribbean and Pacific Group of States (2003), http://www.acpsec.org/gb/press/decrese.htm, 15 May, Brussels.

Ingraham, H. (2001) Chairman's Address to the Opening Ceremony Of The Twenty Second Meeting Of Conference Of Heads Of Government Of The Caribbean Community, 3 July, Nassau, The Bahamas: http://www.caricom.org/pressreleases/pres93_01.htm.

Iqbal, Z. & Khan, M. (1998) *Trade Reform and Regional Integration in Africa,* IMF: Washington.

Kindenberg, U. (2002) 'Most Work in Africa is in the Informal Sector', *National Institute for Working Life Newsletter*, Sweden, 2.

Kumbawa, D. (2002) *Financial Gazette*, Zimbabwe, Harare, 12 June.

Lamy, P. (2003) *Africa, Caribbean, Pacific, Working Together on the Road to Cancun*, Brussels, 1 August 2003, http://europa.eu.int/comm/trade/issues/bilateral/regions/acp/pr010803_en.htm.

Michalopoulos, C. (1998) *The Participation of Developing Countries in the WTO,* World Bank Policy Research Paper Number 1906, http://www.econ.worldbank.org/resource.php?type=5

Michalopoulos, C. (2000) *The Role Of Special And Differential Treatment For Developing Countries In GATT And The*

World Trade Organization, http://www.econ.worldbank.org/docs/1143.pdf

The 'New Partnership for Africa's Development', October 2001, http://www.nepad.org/.

Onguglo, B. & Ito, T. (2003) *How to Make EPA's WTO Compatible? Reforming the Rules on Regional Trade Agreements*, Discussion Paper No.40, European Centre for Development Policy Management.

Pacific ACP Trade Ministers Meeting (2003), *Media Statement,* Forum Secretariat: Nadi, 4 July, http://www.forumsec.org.fj/news/2003/July%2002.htm

Pacific Islands Secretariat Forum, http://www.forumsec.org.fj/

Seneviratne, K. (2000) *Oceania, Pressure on Pacific to Stop Money-laundering,* Online Asia Times, June 29, http://www.atimes.com/oceania/BF29Ah01.html

Schulz, F., et al. (2001). *Regionalisation in a Globalising World,* London & New York, Zed Books.

Thorp, T. (2003) *Enterprise Development in Africa; The African Informal Sector - A Factor Neglected by the NEPAD?* Paper presented to International Conference on Entrepreneurship in Africa: Towards Economic Independence, hosted in 2003 by Namibia Polytechnic, 17-18 September.

Uruguay Round Agreement, Understanding on the Interpretation of Article XXIV of the General Agreement on Tariffs & Trade 1994, http://www.wto.org/english/docs_e/legal_e/10-24_e.htm

US Department of Transportation (2002), *United States, Jamaica Reach Open-Skies Aviation Agreement,* October 30, http://www.dot.gov/affairs/dot09902.htm

WAEMU, Union Economique et Monetaire Ouest Africaine, http://www.uemoa.int/Index.htm

World Trade Organisation, WTO legal texts, http://www.wto.org/english/docs_e/legal_e/legal_e.htm

World Trade Organisation (2003) The 5th WTO Ministerial Conference, Cancun, Mexico, 10 to 14 September 2003, http://www.wto.org/english/thewto_e/minist_e/min03_e/min03_e.htm

Chapter 8

The World Bank, PRSPs and African Poverty

Helen Ware

> *Black Africa is a region united into a single country by its poverty* (Courtemanche 2001).

> *The median African country has the same GDP as a European city of about 50,000 people! ... And the total of OECD agricultural subsidies, at about $300 billion, is equal to Africa's total GDP* (Madavo 2001).

Much has been written on the highly contested issues associated with Africa, the World Bank and indebtedness (Cammack 2003). Even tracking the level of debt is a complex matter (www.jubileeusa.org). In some cases, such as Zambia and Niger, debt relief can actually increase the burden of debt repayment, partly because debtors who were previously prepared to write-off debts as beyond hope of recovery decide to pursue them (www.afrodad.org). Also, it needs to be recognised that the resource requirements of low-income countries extend well beyond debt relief. A reduction by only 10% of current aid flows would offset all of the funding that has been mobilized through debt relief. A 20% cut would offset even a total cancellation of debt service. Yet, since the early 1990s, aid budgets have been declining as a share of OECD GNP. In Sub-Saharan Africa aid receipts have fallen from $32 per capita in 1990 to only $19 by 1998 (Madavo 2001).

This chapter explores some issues concerning one particular, and relatively new, hurdle being presented to African countries: the Poverty Reduction Strategy Papers (PRSP) process. The preparation of these strategies is required by the World Bank, in concert with Western donors, as both a way to keep donors satisfied and engaged and a way to resolve the problems of Africa's poor. The idea is that governments will establish clear strategies to address poverty, resulting from genuine consultation with civil society, and that donors will help to finance these strategies because they are satisfied of both the worthwhile nature of the objectives and the transparency of the accounting.

The nearly four-year old PRSP initiative is the result of the combination of very mixed results of poverty reduction efforts in the 1990's; the need to address the Millennium Development Goals; multilateral funding for debt relief under the Highly Indebted Poor Countries initiatives (HIPC); and a belief that pro-poor policy reforms have failed because conditionalities result in reforms lacking 'ownership' and commitment, while individual projects, however good, tend to weaken commitment and local capacity (Commonwealth Secretariat 2003). So PRSPs have been introduced to replace the old Policy Framework Papers as a basic condition for IMF and World Bank (IDA) concessional lending. They are also a condition for Enhanced HIPC debt relief and are increasingly used by bilateral donors as a focus for improving the quality of aid.

Even in theory, before any messy contact with the realities of life for the poor in Africa, there are many inherent contradictions associated with the PRSP process. It has to be an article of faith that it is possible to pursue growth and poverty reduction together in Africa using very finite resources, otherwise the whole Bank and donor edifice would come tumbling down. Many civil society organizations (CSOs) consider that PRSPs are simply structural adjustment programmes under a new name with poverty reduction as a new layer on top of the old policies (CIDSE in Jadhav 2002: 72). Growth and distribution both matter when it comes to reducing poverty:

> Conventional policies for market restructuring and reform (e.g. liberalization and privatisation) aimed at promoting the development of competitive and efficient markets and economic growth, cannot simply be assumed to be poverty reducing through an anticipated 'trickle-down' process (FAO in Jadhav 2002: 2).

THE MODEL

According to the World Bank, the core PRSP principles are that the strategies should be country-led and owned and based on a broad-spread participatory process. They should also be comprehensive; macro, structural, social, environmental and results-oriented with a long-term perspective, and be costed and prioritised. This is a great deal to ask of countries, which are by definition badly under-resourced, especially since few, if any, of the developed countries have anything of the kind!

The Commonwealth Secretariat (2003) explains that the whole PRSP process is based on three gambles: that governments will take poverty more seriously; that donors will behave better; and that the process will achieve better relations between stakeholders resulting in "increased domestic accountability, more effective aid and better poverty outcomes". There is a constant tension within the model for the PRSPs between economic growth for the nation as a whole and the reduction of poverty for the most disadvantaged sections of the community. Delivering services to remote rural areas has understandably high priority in the consultative processes and helps the poor but does little for national growth unless it can be linked to tourism.

For the IMF/World Bank, "the notion that the right national policy environment is present in poor countries when governments pursue macroeconomic stability, open their economies to the rest of the world and liberalize domestic product and factor markets through privatisation and deregulation" is not to be questioned (Jadhav 2002: 7). This framework focuses only on internal factors, ignoring the role of global forces creating economic crises and poverty in poor countries. A matrix analysis by the European Network on Debt and Development of a sample of 11 PSRFs, (the IMFs equivalent to the PRSPs), 7 of them in Africa, shows how skin-deep the poverty reduction commitment is. All of these PSRFs include privatisations of public utilities and state enterprises and some also include privatisation of state banks, which is likely to reduce the availability of credit to the poor especially in rural areas (EURODAD 2003: 6). Equally all, except Ghana, include trade liberalization measures, and all include some form of fiscal reform with the objective of raising the revenue to GDP ratio generally by raising the rate of VAT, which again could hardly be considered a pro-poor measure.

The fiscal deficit targets of these PRSFs are both unrealistically tight and likely to preclude the use of fiscal policy as a tool of economic policy, especially for the 'good performers' such as Uganda and Tanzania: "[f]undamentally, the desire for, and the unflappable allegiance to, policies of minimal fiscal deficits for all, often hinders poverty reduction spending" (EURODAD 2003: 4). Remarkably, these publicly available plans provide that, should more money than anticipated become available, in none of the countries would this additional money be used for further poverty reduction expenditure. Instead it would be diverted to curb inflation, increase credit for the private sector or build up international reserves; so much for a true poverty focus!

There is little discussion of the time-scale involved in the PRSP process. Accountability requirements call for almost instantaneous results. PRSPs suffer from the "missing-middle – i.e. the grey area between the short term action and long term goals" (European Commission in Jadhav 2002: 31). Thus, countries are supposed to provide annual reports on progress towards poverty reduction targets (prspsynthesis 2003). Yet, even in an ideal world, many measures are not going to produce short-term impacts on poverty, and certainly not within an annual time frame. Expenditure on education is admirable and essential, but it is not going to reduce poverty within the next decade. Further, many critics charge that PRSPs seek to achieve financial stability by curtailing spending in the short term at the expense of increasing economic activity in the longer term (Kalima 2001). The health measures proposed in the PRSPs are equally admirable, but even further removed from having a direct impact on national poverty levels. Strikingly, job creation measures, which could produce a much more rapid impact, are largely ignored. Indeed the PRSPs are "disappointingly meagre" in their coverage of employment issues (ILO in Jadhav 2002: 5). As Germany has acknowledged: "Second-best solutions that work are often more useful in practice than ambitious concepts that can only be implemented with enormous external assistance" (BMZ in Jadhav 2002: 25).

The basic problem with the PRSP model is that it is based on the core assumption that 'correct' economic policy and budgetary planning, following World Bank/IMF guidelines, will resolve poverty. The old paradigm of the Washington Consensus still flourishes. Indeed, in many cases the old adjustment instruments and targets have reappeared, as ACTION AID (in Jadhav 2002: 64) says "new form, same substance and same impact, on the working poor and the excluded".

Critics of the World Bank have variously attributed its proclaimed commitment to poverty reduction to empty rhetoric, hypocrisy, incompetence, confusion, or overload in the absence of a coherent agenda. The commitment is genuine, but it is not a first order goal: poverty reduction is an intended consequence of its principle objective, the transformation of social and governmental relations and institutions in the developing world in order to generalize and facilitate capitalist accumulation on a global scale, and build capitalist hegemony through the promotion of tightly controlled forms of 'participation' and 'ownership' (Cammack 2003). It is not that the World Bank is engaged in some sort of plot; it is simply fulfilling its role as a Northern donor-sponsored bank, largely staffed by economists who know nothing but the neo-liberal agenda.

At a very practical level, poverty analysis is improved through the PRSP process, but the policy detail often has limited poverty focus and fails to incorporate a critical review of past failures, while implementation is seriously limited by enduring weaknesses in budget and public-sector management (Commonwealth Secretariat 2003). These management weaknesses cannot be fixed by simple capacity building exercises because they are the systematic result of basic cultural factors. Domestic accountability remains very weak; not helped by the fact that the participatory processes largely bypass formal political institutions. In many cases this is necessary because political leaders are actively opposed to the neo-liberal economic paradigm on which the whole PRSP process is based. Civil society often starts with unreasonably high initial expectations and rapidly becomes disillusioned. Many PRSPs simply fall short of setting out a strong national strategy with clear priorities and good sector policies. Where PRSPs are associated with strong moves towards decentralisation there is the further problem that planning, which already strongly challenges the capacities of central governments, is simply beyond the capacity of local authorities. Finally, "partners supporting PRSPs will continue to face a dilemma of strengthening the poverty impact of policy *versus* encouraging a good country-specific process" (Commonwealth Secretariat 2003: 26).

In relation to the good governance goal it is hardly surprising that the PRSPs fall short: "this agenda is far too long for the governments of poor countries to approach with clarity, commitment, or reasonable expectations. Indeed, the good governance imperative might be more reasonable if it were recast as good enough governance" (Grindle 2003: 11). Yet, if government is not made to work for the people, and if corruption is not controlled, nothing is really going to change.

Ownership

Ownership by the recipients is a new mantra with donors. Indeed, many would argue that without ownership, there can be no successful development. Past failures are blamed on the lack of ownership. Explaining the flaws in earlier structural adjustment programs, Jean-Louis Sarbib (2000), the outgoing World Bank Vice President for Africa, explained that governments had been insincere; "these people were signing on the dotted line, saying we will reform, but they knew reforming would undermine their own positions of privilege". To quote his successor "we need to create space for people to participate in the making of the future of their country". This goal is articulated in the Comprehensive Development Framework which "is centred around a few key principles: country ownership and leadership – partnership – participation – coordination – comprehensiveness" (Madavo 2002). The problem for the Bank staff is that they need to secure 'ownership' of an agenda which has already been set in concert with the IMF, and which allows countries some freedom on the choice of poverty reduction measures, but minimal choice in economic policy where governments must include privatization, deregulation, budgetary constraints and trade and financial liberalization.

The question also arises as to whose ownership is being required. African governments are required to have a certain level of ownership, otherwise the PRSP process would never get off the ground. Yet, the process also lays great stress on consultation with stakeholders throughout the community, even representatives of the poor themselves. To require this actually requires more of African governments than the donors require of themselves. It also leaves unanswered the key question of how differences of perspective and opinion are to be resolved. If an elected government wishes to move in one direction and civil society chooses another, is the Bank to have the casting vote ? What weight is to be given to the views of divergent groups within civil society?

The Bank reports three examples where civil society's priorities resulted in alterations to the national PRSP:

- In Mauritania – new discussion of judicial reform, decentralization of health services;
- In Tanzania – the abolition of primary school fees, and employment creation schemes for the poor;

- In Guinea – better delivery of services to the remote areas of the country (Madavo 2002).

It is interesting that, of the three examples, only the Tanzanian Case (discussed further below) demonstrably involves a significant change in government expenditure, the remainder are far more nebulous requirements and none of these measures effects macro-economic policy.

As a measure of a less donor-driven process, the European Union allows recipient governments to nominate 3 priority sectors for their European Development Fund Assistance (without necessarily consulting civil society), only 7 African countries have nominated education even as a third priority, which, as the European Parliament's Committee on Development and Co-Operation noted, is very different to donor and civil society priorities (see 'Education in the Context of Poverty Reduction in Developing Countries': Public Hearing, European Parliament, Brussels, 18/03/03). Thus, given free scope, government priorities appear to be very different from those found in the PRSPs where education looms very large.

Since governments have to go through the PRSP process if they wish to secure access to debt relief and new donor funding they are effectively being forced into 'ownership'. In many contexts, governments are now more accountable to donors than to their constituents (OECD in Jadhav 2002: 37). As a consequence, much of the World Bank's reportage of African ownership of the PRSP process has all the conviction of the dancing-bear owner with a whip assuring the RSPCA that 'of course, the bear really enjoys dancing'.

As a solution, "[a]ctive steps need to be taken by the donor community (including the IFIs) to allow partner governments the space to develop home-grown solutions" (Strategic Partnership with Africa in Jadhav 2002: 39). As it is, reading the African PRSPs one is struck by how rare it is to come across any proposals which have a distinctively African flavour or any tinge of novelty. Even the donors consider that "more innovative and rigorous thinking is needed on conceptualising alternative, more flexible post-stabilization macro frameworks" (DFID in Jadhav 2002: 47).

The Nature of Planning

The very idea of a planned economy is supposed to be irredeemably out of date. So what are these poor African governments actually supposed to be doing? They are supposed to be strategizing. Common features of the PRSPs are that they "focus on enhanced expenditure programs (especially in health, education, water and sanitation, and roads and infrastructure); institutional reforms to improve governance (such as decentralization, civil service reform, tax reform); and structural reforms (including trade reform, privatisation, financial sector reform and agriculture sector reform) (prspsynthesis 2003).

World Bank staff are uncomfortable with politics. In their world-view there is a single correct solution to each economic problem. PRSPs contain little, if any, discussion of options. Staff wish to suggest that it is possible to promote a wide international convergence of public policy around the mantra of global integration and social inclusion within a technical and legal framework that rides roughshod over issues of politics and the shaping of the economy; ignoring the practical day-to-day world in which policies have to be made to work on the ground.

For Uganda, Craig and Porter (2002) have shown just how counter-productive this can be. In the context of decentralization and local governments being diverted from true political debate, "national and local political authorities are reformed and narrowed down to focus on the plethora of financial stability and integration best practice 'rules' considered necessary for the 'accountable' delivery of resources to areas of local need according to globally determined standards" (Craig & Porter 2002). As the OECD recognises, "an excessive focus by external assistance agencies on the technocratic aspects of PRSP to the detriment of political determinants, may erode, and perhaps ultimately compromise, development effectiveness" (OECD in Jadhav 2002:35).

Some requirements of the PRSP process are very clear: governments are supposed to sell off state enterprises and reduce the size of the public sector. Much of the language about right sizing the public service is very loose. So loose that it is not normally clear whether the teachers and nurses who are supposed to be providing invaluable services to the poor are to be counted as public servants or not. This is despite the fact that they would often form the absolute majority of public servants if included. In Uganda between 1990 and 1997 the numbers on the Government's payroll reduced by more than half from 320,00 to 147,000. In the late 1990s Tanzania 'released' 145,000 public servants from government employment (from an original total of about 355,000) in response to IMF conditionalities and was then left to ponder why white-collar poverty was so widespread. Yet, despite these measures neither country managed to lower the wages bill because the reduction in staff numbers was more than offset by real rises in the pay levels, to reverse the steep erosion in the previous decade (Donors Working Group on Public Service Reform 2002).

For both teachers and nurses it is actually easy to calculate how many will be needed using simple ratios based on class-sizes or the numbers of patients who can plausibly be assisted per hour. Yet, PRSPs do not appear to use these simplest of estimates. This is no oversight, it is a deliberate omission because the answers are too uncomfortable. If, for simplicity, the ratio of 1 teacher per 30 pupils is used (putting primary and secondary loads together and including some teacher/administrators) and half of the population is under age 15, as is commonplace in Africa, then simple arithmetic decrees that, on average, for every group of 15-20 working-age adults, the government must, at least, be able to collect enough taxes to pay the salary of a teacher. Even this assumes that both women and men are equally engaged in the labour force and that everyone is gainfully employed which is quite unrealistic. Furthermore, the calculation takes no account of the impact of AIDS taking sick people and carers alike out of the labour force. Even if education is privatised, and perhaps handed over to the churches, individuals still have to produce a sufficient surplus to pay teachers. In some countries teachers may be overpaid in terms of the ratio between their salaries and per capita GNP, but teachers do have a level of basic expenses above those of peasant farmers. And all this is just for schooling without considering paying health, police, agricultural extension or other essential workers.

For education, health care or any other universal service, the basic issue is that the African economies have to be able to produce a surplus sufficient to pay for their recurrent costs. To take one quite simple case – it is highly doubtful whether a country such as Malawi produced such a surplus even before the impact of AIDS. There is no sustainable level of debt repayment for Malawi because Malawi does not produce enough even to meet the core basic needs of its population.

AIDS

The impact of HIV/AIDS is yet another area where there is a basic conflict between theory and reality. Certainly the PRSP documents include a chapter on health in which AIDS looms large, but the remainder of the plans tend to rest on the premise that life will go on as before without any impact from AIDS. To cite one example, Zambia is estimated to have an adult prevalence rate for HIV/AIDS of 20%, which means that there are some 870,000 people in Zambia currently living with HIV/AIDS. Clearly, with rates at these levels, everyone in Zambia is daily having to cope with the reality of HIV/AIDS if not for themselves, for a spouse, sibling or fellow employee if not for all 3. One study in Zambia found that for two thirds of those families where the father died of AIDS, disposable income dropped by 80% or more in the first year. Of the urban fatherless families, 61% moved to cheaper housing, 39% lost their access to piped water; and 21% of girls and 17% of boys dropped out of school (Nampanya-Serpell 2001). Such a reality must also impact on any realistic vision of the future for the Zambian economy. It is difficult to envisage tourists flocking to such a country, and AIDS is literally decimating the rural labour force, yet tourism and agriculture are set out as the growth industries in the Zambian PRSP.

It should be recognised that the weakness of PRSPs in addressing HIV/AIDS is not a reflection of ignorance by the countries themselves or at the World Bank. The Bank's own publications (eg Bonnel 2000) show that for 80 developing countries the negative impact on per capita GDP growth due to HIV/AIDS rises consistently from 0.6% per annum at a HIV prevalence rate of 5% to 1.4% per annum at a prevalence rate of 30%. Another study shows that in Botswana, from 2000 to 2010, even though the overall economic growth rate will remain positive, due to HIV/AIDS the proportion of households living in poverty will rise from 38% to 45% and the average per capita income for the poorest quartile will fall by 13% (Bollinger & Stover 1999). For the Ivory Coast, household survey evidence shows just how far families living with AIDS are forced both to reduce per capita consumption and to move into disavings mode. One might argue with some of the detailed figures, but clearly there is no shortage of relevant information available (UNAIDS & UNDP 2000).

The problem is not a lack of information, it is a problem of compartmentalisation, leaving HIV/AIDS to the chapter on health (with a nod to the issue under education/teacher supply), and of Ministries of Finance and World Bank/ IMF finance officials not having a broad enough perspective (though they may describe death as a 'disutility to the individual', as several World Bank staffers have repeated in slide presentations available on www.worldbank.org). AIDS needs to figure with conviction in every chapter of the PRSP. For example, in the education chapter, planning needs to be on the basis that up to 10% of teachers are likely to die of AIDS. Zambia already loses almost as many teachers to AIDS each year as it manages to train new entrants to the profession. Thus, in 1999, 1,600 teachers, or 1 teacher in 20, died of AIDS. Beyond the economic impact of lost investment in training, and the creation of orphaned teachers' children, it is chilling to imagine the psychological impact that such a toll must be having on Zambian school children (Nampanya-Serpell 2001). To plan for the future one must be able to envisage a viable future rather than a long-drawn-out death.

ALICE IN WORLD BANK LAND

AIDS provides only one example of the disjunction between reality and the PRSP formula. In the Interim PRSP for the Democratic Republic of Congo, "where natural resources are plentiful, heavily exploited, and directly linked to the perpetuation of civil conflict", minerals and petroleum are only mentioned in passing as principle exports. Some 80% of GDP in DRC from 1990-1999 was derived from the export of mining products yet, "the role of natural resources in relation to the conflict is raised only in reference to the plunder of foreign occupying forces, [while] the potential development of these sectors to generate economic growth for poverty reduction is not addressed" (Stites 2003: 4).

For Zambia, the whole PRSP is based on a vastly over-optimistic view of the future of the local copper mining industry. The strategy even includes a discussion of how to open a new copper mine under phase 2. The Joint Staff Assessment (JSA of IMF/ World Bank staff) cautions against reliance on copper, but has to mute its comments or risk demolishing any scenario on which Zambia can attain a positive per capita economic growth rate.

Conflict and Surrealism

Understandably, explaining how the government is going to reduce poverty in countries where large tracts of land are not under the government's control frequently results in splendidly surrealist prose. Thus, for example, the JSA for Sierra Leone notes in passing that any growth strategy will depend on the government takeover of the mining areas from the rebels! The Sierra Leone PRSP includes the standard proposals for creating a business environment more attractive to foreign investors and for providing micro-credit, this time to allow refugees and internally displaced persons to become small-scale diamond miners; the success of which is to be measured by an indicator of the "value of official diamond exports", as if the Kimberley Process Certification Scheme is about to take over in up-country Sierra Leone. Paradoxically, there is no discussion of the role of diamonds in financing the continuing fighting (Pegg 2003).

Remarkably, the World Bank sees the first challenge of debt relief as the need to extend decisions under the HIPC framework to more countries that are eligible "in particular by accommodating the special circumstances of countries that are emerging from conflict such as the Democratic Republic of Congo" (Madavo 2001). This approach would suggest that in the World Bank's eyes, the odd civil war is not so much a blot on the copybook than evidence of a tendency to independent thought on economic policy.

It is disturbing, since Uganda is often quoted as having a model PRSP (even by the IMF Executive Board), that the documentation for Uganda skirts around continuing fighting in that country and the military expenditure necessary to maintain a semblance of order in the North. The European Commission commented on this in their Assessment of the PRSP noting that there was to be a commitment to maintain defence expenditure within 2 per cent of GDP. The plan was that expenditure on law and order was also to decline significantly, but this was clearly dependent upon being able to achieve the security targets in terms of a reduction in casualties and people forced to flee their homes.

For all countries, irrespective of their current experience of conflict, budgetary planning needs to take account of the impact of military expenditure upon poverty. Transparency in budgeting and accountability to civil society is a fiction unless military expenditure is included. Donors who attack developing countries for financial irresponsibility still continue to sell them vastly expensive arms. In 2002 Britain sold Tanzania a military radar system for 28 million pounds; a sum that could have provided basic healthcare for 2 million people or education for 3.5 million children. The House of Lords is now trying to get development sustainability considered before arms sales are approved, as formally required by the European Union (Ahmed 2002). However, not all military expenditure is necessarily poverty inducing. While buying military equipment on credit from the first world has a very negative impact on the poor of Africa, paying modest wages to large numbers of otherwise unemployable young men (and some young women) could actually reduce poverty, depending on the training provided and how these wages were financed.

Another surreal feature of the PRSPs is their failure to prioritise and most especially their failure to give priority to those reforms that deliver the most benefit to poor people. The 'wish-list' is alive and well but remains meaningless; governments have to make strategic choices. It is not enough to have each government ministry with social responsibilities, such as education, health and infrastructure, compile their own PRSP chapter. There has to be an overarching vision of what needs to be accomplished and in what order and of where limited funds can have the greatest impact. Without such a vision, there is a risk that civil society involvement will only serve to legitimise non-poverty reducing policies.

CORRUPTION

A minor change in language can produce remarkable results. Discussing corruption may well be regarded as offensive especially where the implication is that this is a vice never found in industrial countries (as if ENRON did not overshadow anything Africa could produce). However, transparency is an acceptable requirement and thus, the Cameroon PRSP, for example, discusses audits of the petroleum industry and the need to 'promote transparency' in this area.

What is not discussed is just how easily the Bank's economic prescriptions can be derailed by corruption, nor whether they could ever be made to work under African conditions. One Nigerian NGO made a submission to the World Bank/IMF arguing that corruption eradication should be prioritised over poverty eradication for Africa as the one best way of assisting the poor. Local studies have shown just how onerous corruption is for individuals striving to survive at the grass-roots level (African Citizens Development Foundation in Jadhav 2002: 118). Privatisation of state enterprises raises severe risks of corruption even in industrialised countries. For example, in Malawi corrupt management selling off grain stocks left people starving. Corruption thus, provides a good example where it would be eminently sensible to have a draft PRSP chapter, ready for adapting to national circumstances, but which would serve as a baseline for best practice in defining matters such as the need to publish government ministers and officials' salaries and benefits.

UGANDA: THE PRSP SUCCESS

Uganda is widely considered to be a success story showing how governments, banks and donors can work together to create an economic climate conducive to economic growth and poverty reduction: "Uganda has achieved an unprecedented joining-up of poverty eradication plans, corresponding budgets, negotiated agreements and the extraordinary focus of resources around a common sense of purpose in the PRSP framework" (Craig & Porter 2002). In a considerable achievement, real per capita GDP rose by nearly 4% per annum during the 1990s (before the PRSP) and the estimated proportion of the population living below the basic needs poverty line fell from 55% in 1992 to 35% in 1999 (Appleton 2001).

Uganda produced a draft Poverty Eradication Action Plan (PEAP) in 1997 and donors treated this as Uganda's PRSP enabling Uganda to be the first African country to reach the 'completion point' for enhanced HIPC debt relief in May 2000. The Ugandan PEAP had 4 general goals: fast and sustainable economic growth and structural transformation; good governance and security; increasing the ability of the poor to raise their incomes; and increasing the quality of life for the poor. Being the darling of the donors to some extent made Uganda's continuing economic success a self-fulfilling prophecy. Net official aid flows to Uganda were some US$800 million in 2001 representing

US$37 per person and 13% of GNI. HIPC debt relief to Uganda from 1999 to 2000 was US$1,300 million (for Tanzania it was US$2,000 million). Uganda's PRGF shows that Uganda plans to spend 7.7% of GDP on social sector expenditure of which 4% would be for education, only 0.1% is to be spent on improving agriculture.

A Less Successful Case: Zambia

Zambia makes an interesting and contrasting case study of the development of a PRSP. The country has not suffered a civil war and it has a semi-democratic government; although views on the 2001 national elections are widely divergent and calling the President a 'cabbage' is apparently still a criminal offence (Civil Society for Poverty Reduction 2002). As far back as 1990, Zambia's Foreign Minister, Mavis Muvunda, told the United Nations that constant debt servicing "translates into a dehumanising life of poverty, malnutrition, infant mortality and moral degradation" (*UN Chronicle* 27: 22). Equally, Zambia is not one of the showcase PRSP countries (such as Uganda, Tanzania or Mozambique). Anyone who has access to the Internet can read Zambia's PRSP alongside those of the other countries participating in the process. To quote the World Bank's Glossary:

> PRSPs describe a country's macroeconomic, structural and social policies and strategies and programs to promote growth and reduce poverty, as well as associated external funding needs. PRSPs are prepared by governments through a participatory process involving civil society and development partners.

Zambia's PRSP is a document of 17 chapters, 29 Appendices and 197 pages. And yet, it is still remarkable for its lack of analytical content and insights. It is a turgid and uninspiring document. Sometimes it is impossible to tell whether one is reading a misprint or its compilers were so intent on working their way through an imposed formula that they had no concern for its accuracy or meaning. Thus, for example, in the Executive Summary (which was presumably proof read several times) there is the statement in the third paragraph that: "[t]he majority of the people suffer from weak purchasing power, homelessness and insufficient access to basic necessities such as education, health, food, and clean water". Despite this there is minimal further discussion of housing needs or nutritional statistics!

It is estimated that "around 73% of Zambians are classified as poor. Poverty is more prevalent in rural areas compared to the urban areas (83% and 56% respectively), but it has risen faster in the urban areas lately due to failing industries and rising unemployment" (Zambian PRSP: 10). However, it is very difficult to know exactly what this means since the information provided is that "poverty can be defined in the Zambian context as lack of access to such things as freely determined consumption of goods and services, shelter and other basic needs of life". Rural poverty is "largely attributed to poorly functioning markets for agricultural output and to low agricultural productivity because of reliance on very basic implements as well as low utilisation of agricultural inputs". Urban poverty, apart from the decline in mining, also reflects the fact that since 1995, eighty-six percent of jobs in the manufacturing sector have been lost.

One positive feature of the Zambian PRSP is its realism in discussing economic growth rates, which it sees as being no higher than 4% per annum in the immediate future. Yet, to achieve poverty reduction, rates would need to be in the range of 5-8% per annum. Population growth is 1.9% per annum even with AIDS. Zambia's PRGF shows that even if all plans are fulfilled only 2.2% of GDP is to be spent on social expenditure. This compares with an average target of 9.1% for the eleven countries in the EURODAD matrix. Remarkably, Zambia is to encourage large-scale agriculture farming with commercial agriculture slated to take over from copper mining: "[t]he list of known agricultural products where Zambia has both comparative and competitive advantage includes coffee, cotton, groundnuts, flowers, paprika". Great hope is attached to extending agriculture, and even to the opening up of new agricultural blocks. Sadly, there is no discussion of how access to new areas will be handled without corruption or ethnic favouritism. The issue of the promotion of the World Bank's views on the individualization of communal land tenure in the African PRSPs merits a study to itself.

One very practical problem that donors face is that they have to decide whether a country is overall performing in a manner which means that its government is acceptable for debt relief or not. In this cut-off decision there is little room for nuanced presentations. Thus, USAID's *2004 Congressional Budget Justification for Zambia* in part reads as follows:

> since 1991, Zambia has undergone a political transition from decades of one-party autocracy to multi-party democracy. Although much remains to be done, fundamental economic liberalization and structural reform programs have accompanied this political transformation. A more politically balanced parliament is struggling to assert itself following decades of subjugation by the Executive Branch, while a poorly resourced judiciary is seeking to strengthen the independence and efficiency of the legal system.

It is unclear what USAID could or would have done if multi-party democracy had failed to deliver 'fundamental economic liberalization'. Sometimes donors can become hostages to their own rhetoric, and the PRSP model certainly requires that all recipient governments accept donors' views on the path to economic progress.

The most recent development concerning Zambia's relationship to the international financial institutions is that, on August 1, 2003, the IMF and the Zambian government issued a joint statement announcing that Zambia will not be able to reach the completion point for HIPC debt relief in December 2003 as scheduled because the Government cannot reach the benchmarks required. Zambia is faced with 4 Structural Performance Criteria, and 9 Structural Benchmarks, which means that it faces an exceptionally high level of conditionality even by African standards (EURODAD 2003: 7). Basically, the problem relates to the wages and housing allowances bill for public servants which is projected to be about K500 billion or 2.5% of GDP above the 2003 budgeted amount of K1, 520 billion (IMF 2003). The government is still negotiating with the public service unions but it is in a bind because it is dependent upon their political support. Meanwhile the money is not available for poverty reduction priorities (Civil Society for Poverty Reduction 2003).

The last, and perhaps also the first, fact to be noted about Zambia is that average life expectancy at birth is now a mere 37 years. This for a country that had attained a life expectancy in the upper 60s! Given an AIDS impact at this extreme level it must be very hard to think in terms of economic planning as the solution to the country's most important problems. Perhaps part of the reason why planning for the Ugandan economy is proving more successful is simply that the expectation of life there is ten years longer at 47 years.

School Fees and User Pays

One way of drawing a case study from the overwhelming body of PRSP e-resources is to examine an individual country or geographic region. Another is to examine how a single issue is treated across a number of national PRSPs. Education is vital both to promote growth and reduce poverty in Africa (Appiah & MacMahon 2002). In this context, the treatment of school fees provides a very interesting example of the interaction between national budgeting, the World Bank and African and Northern civil society movements.

The World Bank, apparently drawing upon Latin American experience, for some 15 years favoured school fees (and other user pays systems). For education, the Bank's argument was that charging such fees gives parents ownership, generates community support and ensures that quality services can be delivered in the schools. Schools are in a better position to collect fees than local governments are to collect taxes because the children need to attend on a regular basis and schools have the ultimate if difficult sanction of excluding children whose payments are in arrears.

However, the World Bank's official policy, heavily influenced by lobbying by developed country NGOs, is now that "[t]he World Bank does not support user fees for primary education and for basic health services for poor people" (www.worldbank.org).

This reflects a recent conversion: Tanzania proposed to impose school fees as recently as February 1999 at the instigation of the World Bank and the IMF. Yet by July 1999, World Bank President, James Wolfensohn, was assuring the United States Congress that user fees were no longer an issue and he would look into specific cases raised. In 2000, Congress enacted an addition to aid legislation, which requires the U.S. representative to the World Bank to vote against projects, or loans that include fees for primary education or health care.

Now, as of early 2003, the World Bank has gone further and says that it will 'actively oppose' user fees for primary education although the paper setting out this policy is still in draft form (Global Campaign for Education 2003). Ruth Kagia, the World Bank's Director of Education, says that the definition of fees to be opposed will include textbook charges, compulsory uniforms, PTA fees, or 'community contributions', and school-based activity fees such as exam fees. This is because the Bank now accepts that all of these charges are a barrier to access and the completion of primary education. Yet, at the same time, the Bank still supports private sector investment in basic services arguing that the state has the responsibility to fund, but not necessarily to deliver, basic education. It is thus hardly surprising that civil society organizations in rural Africa find it hard to understand the Bank's policies on user pays.

The World Bank formally abandoned its support for school fees because of the impact of American civil society organizations working upon the US Congress, not because of the views of developing countries or their CSOs, suggesting that there exists:

> A knowledge gap between northern and southern CSOs regarding reform of IFIs which reflects the organizational structure of the Bank and the Fund. This in turn, reflects the real-world balance of power. Consequently, CSOs in G-7 countries are able to exercise more political pressure over the international financial institutions than governments and CSOs in low-income countries where the projects and policies are actually implemented and the effects felt. This fundamental imbalance distorts every Fund and Bank undertaking, the PRSP notwith-standing (Bread for the World Institute in Jadhav 2002: 67).

So having been prodded by the World Bank to impose fees through an education levy in 1999; and still 'assisted ' by the Bank, Tanzania abolished primary school fees in January 2002. The result was that "school enrolments have doubled. 1.5 million kids turned up in school. Classrooms are bursting at the seams. Unless Tanzania gets the kind of urgent support from donors that it needs, this bold initiative could end in frustration" (Phil Twyford, Oxfam quoted allAfrica.com 22 April 2002). As one of the World Bank Education For All Fast Track Initiative countries, the objective for Tanzania, once accountability systems are in place, is actually that donors and the Bank should provide U$10 per child to the schools for primary education. Earlier evidence from Uganda showed that, of each dollar allocated for education, only 10 cents reached the school, now the proportion is said by the President to be 90 cents (World Bank Education for All Video Conference, December 13, 2001).

School fees are highly contentious politically. Governments that abolish them gain great political popularity. In 2003, President Mwai Kibaki of Kenya campaigned on the issue of abolishing primary school fees, and school enrolments rose by 20% in the week after school fees were abolished. One of the biggest groups to benefit from this was Kenya's estimated 1.2 million AIDS orphans. Parents of children with disabilities often keep them at home if fees have to be found but send them to school once they are abolished. Children in the drought stricken areas also benefited, but in some cases in Baringo and Turkana they only attended school where meals were also provided otherwise they would have to go foraging for food and hunting.

When Malawi abolished its very modest school fees together with the school uniform requirements in 1994, primary enrolment soared by almost 50% (Government of Malawi and UNICEF 1998). Again, when Uganda eliminated school fees the primary enrolment rate rose from 50% to 90%. In Burkina Faso, as part of the PRSP process, school fees have been waived for girls in an effort to overcome the longstanding discrimination against them. There is no question that abolishing school fees increases access to education for the poorest and most disadvantaged groups in society.

However, 'free education' is still highly expensive for government budgets. The estimated cost of abolishing school fees to the government of Kenya is $137 million for a school year. For Burkina Faso the government has pledged to devote 20% of its total budget to education by 2010 in the hopes of having 70% of children in school by that date. The vital question is where the governments are going to find the money to fund their education budgets. If schools are not charging fees then schools have to be funded through the taxation system or through donor funding; and for education the major costs are recurrent costs each year not the one-off commitments for capital expenditure preferred by donors. In the Kenyan case, the government will provide the majority of the cost with the remainder coming from the World Bank and bi-lateral donors (Adler 2003). Such a funding pattern then places children's education at the mercy of their national government being able to maintain harmonious relations with the Bank and donors.

To take the case of Burkina Faso, if the government does spend 20% of its total budget on education, a simple calculation would imply that each adult worker has to pay at least one quarter of a schoolteacher's salary in taxes (recognising that only a fifth of total taxation is going to teachers' salaries). In a poor country with very few rich people to assist with ameliorating the taxation burden, and where the majority of rural farmers would have incomes well below a primary school teacher's salary, this is clearly going to pose a significant problem.

Arguments over charging user fees for health services are similar to those relating to school fees; although there is a much higher quality literature on health fees (see *The Lancet* or *British Medical Journal*). However, one might expect that even the most extreme economic rationalist might query the rationality of charging fees for the treatment of infectious diseases. Charging fees at Nairobi's Special Clinic for Sexually Transmitted Diseases resulted in a 40% decrease in attendance by men and 65% by women over a nine-month period!

Water and sanitation are closely linked to health status and raise even more complex issues concerning user fees. Zambia has privatised urban water supplies only to find that people cannot afford to pay enough for water to allow for investments in repairs and extensions of the system. Guinea and Malawi had similar experiences. In a sad irony, the end result is that clean water is available, at least in the towns, but, since people cannot afford to pay their bills, they go back to using contaminated wells or resort to 'stealing' water from golf-course irrigation systems

The arguments related to user fees are a good example of just how complex the public debates over just one issue within the PRSPs can be. How realistic is it to expect that the whole content of these documents will be subject to informed public examination? For the Zambian PRSP there is a user-friendly version, which includes a discussion of how to enable illiterate adults to access its contents, but even it baulks at explaining the economic theory on which the process is based or translating the economic technical terms into the local languages (Civil Society for Poverty Reduction 2002).

DECENTRALIZATION

> A Ugandan villager goes to market to sell a pig. First he has to pay for a movement permit from the local council, then a permit from a vet. When he gets to market, he has to pay market entry, and finally – if he actually sells the pig – a tax on its sale. Then the cycle starts again. The person who bought the pig pays a purchase tax, as well as the movement permit to take the pig from the market to his or her own village (Ellis & James 2002: 1).

The World Bank has a positively romantic attachment to the virtues of decentralization. The Tanzanian popular version of the PRSP document has a cartoon showing the central government as a father saying to local government as son: "[s]on, I'm giving you more power to decide what you think is best for your regions" to which the son replies: "[t]hanks dad, that will also leave you a chance to concentrate on major issues" (quoted in Cammack 2003). Some 89% of the early PRSPs had fiscal decentralization on the agenda (User's Guide: note 5). There appears to be a belief that regimes, which are notoriously corrupt at a central government level, suddenly become squeaky-clean at the local level. Hence, the belief that user fees will actually be used to provide services.

Research suggests far otherwise. Intensive research on individual households in 9 villages in Uganda and 10 subvillages in Tanzania in 2001 measured how villagers gradually escape poverty, and discovered that local taxation now virtually blocks this process of trading up from chickens to goats to cattle to land; or from cash from non-farm income to farm inputs to higher farm income to land or to livestock:

> For Uganda, fiscal decentralisation has meant the imposition on local rural populations of a dense thicket of commodity, market, sales and transit taxes. These taxes are impenetrable to comprehend by the ordinary citizen; they are collected by private tenderers often in a climate of intimidation and coercion; they are only partly passed onto revenue offices; the proportion that is sent in is spent largely on elected councillors' emoluments; and they fail to achieve any proper connection in the minds of citizens between taxes levied and services delivered (Ellis & James 2002: 10).

Tanzania is less advanced down a similar decentralisation path, but also faces the imposition of bad taxes that "distort relative prices, discourage market development, scare away traders, and add unreasonable costs to productive enterprises "(Ellis & James 2002: 15). One wonders where the amazing notion of privatising tax collection came from, does no one at the Bank read any history? Very sadly, the end result is that decentralization of government and services becomes an additional burden keeping the rural poor in poverty.

Conclusion: Some Thoughts on Action

The PRSP model assumes that there is a direct linear relationship between economic growth and decreasing poverty. While the countries of black Africa stand in dire need of economic growth, overall there is no guarantee that this will feed into poverty reduction. It is most unusual and cheering to see that the PRSP for Guinea lists the 7 largest mining companies in Guinea and the revenues which they provide to the central government, the extent of their investment in local development and the number of jobs created (directly or indirectly) by each enterprise. Chad actually has a law, passed in 1998, which allocates the majority of oil revenues "to the priority sectors involved in poverty reduction" and provides "tools to monitor and supervise" the use of these funds (Chad I-PRSP 2000: para 70).

However many problems one may have with the whole PRSP process, it is important to recognise that for the major donors and financers it is now THE game in town and it is therefore important to consider whether, however flawed the system, it is worthwhile engaging with it for those things which it may be able to deliver. Since consultations with civil society will continue can these mechanisms be used to secure better outcomes for the poor? One remediable defect of the process is the way it separates civil society from the official democratic processes. Even the World Bank acknowledges that "we need to pay particular attention to ensuring that Parliaments are adequately involved, to ensure that participation does not result in disempowering elected Governments and Parliaments" yet, in the next breath the Bank is proposing that "Parliaments could vote each year, as part of their budget laws, on a set of short-term actions required to implement the PRSP. This could be the basis for balance of payment and programmatic support" (Madavo 2002). So much for Parliaments deciding how their countries should be governed!

Of all the complaints against the PRSP process, the most common is "the deliberate lack of involvement of parliamentarians in countries' poverty reduction strategies" (Southern CSOs in Jadhav 2002: 79). UNCTAD (2002: 16) has even expressed concern that under PRSPs the "[s]ubstitution of conventional institutions of representative democracy by ad hoc mechanisms involving some segments of civil society could, paradoxically, undermine the fledgling institutions of representative democracy taking root in African societies". Perhaps Parliamentarians' groups (e.g. through the Commonwealth) could work with African parliamentarians to develop the information networks and tools to re-insert them into the process.

Another area for action is through major Western companies that deal with African governments. Corruption flourishes in the dark and if such companies are transparent about their dealings, this vastly reduces the potential for politicians and their friends and relations to take the cream off the system. For example, pressure should be brought to bear on oil companies to support the international 'Publish What you Pay' campaign by publicly disclosing, in a disaggregated, regular and timely manner, all net taxes, fees, royalties and other payments made to African states, at any level, or to local communities, including compensation payments and community development funding (Catholic Relief services 2003). Sub-Saharan governments will receive over $200 billion in oil revenues over the next decade. It is vital that this money does not go astray and that other countries learn from Nigeria's malign experience.

For those who have an interest in the fate of Africa's poor, the national PRSPs of which there are now nearly 20 at various stages, are an invaluable resource. However imperfect they are, they contain a unique range of instantly available information on the extent and nature of poverty in Africa and what national governments say they intend to do about it. Anyone researching in this area needs to use this resource; even if their final conclusion is that trade is to be preferred to aid or debt relief, and that therefore the European Commission's 'Everything but Arms' initiative to allow duty-free, quota-free access for all products from all least developed countries into the European Union is likely to deliver a much more sustainable benefit to the poorest than any number of PRSPs.

References

Adler, L. (2003) in *The East African Standard*, 10th May.

Ahmed, K. (2002) 'British Arms Sales to Africa Soar', *The Observer,* 3rd February.

Appiah, E. & McMahon, W. (2002) 'The Social Outcome of Education and Feedbacks on Growth in Africa', *Journal of Development Studies,* 38(14), pp. 27-42.

Appleton, S. (2001) *Poverty Reduction During Growth: The Case of Uganda, 1992-2000,* University of Nottingham, http://www.uppap.or.ug/docs/simonpaper.pdf

Bollinger, L. & Stover, J. (1999), *The Economic Impact of AIDS in Botswana,* The Futures Group, http://www.policyproject.com/pubs/SEImpact/botswana.pdf

Bonnel, R. (2000) *ADF Background Paper, Economic Impacts of HIV/AIDS,* World Bank, ACT Africa.

Cammack, P. (2003) 'What the World Bank Means by Poverty Reduction', Paper presented to *Staying Poor: Chronic Poverty and Development Policy Conference*, Chronic Poverty Research Centre, University of Manchester.

Catholic Relief Services (2003), *Bottom of the Barrel: Africa's Oil Boom and the Poor,* New York.

Civil Society for Poverty Reduction (Zambia) (2002) *The Path away from Poverty: An Easy Look at Zambia's Poverty Reduction Strategy Paper 2002-2004,* CAFRAD.

Civil Society for Poverty Reduction (Zambia) (2003) *Press Release,* 27th August.

Civil Society for Poverty Reduction (2002) *Governance in Zambia: A Civil Society Perspective* for the Consultative Group Meeting, 7 July, Lusaka.

Civil Society for Poverty Reduction (2003) *Analysis of the Participatory Provincial Poverty Monitoring,* www.sarpn.org.za

Commonwealth Secretariat. (2003) PRSP Learning Event, 9 July.

Courtemanche, G. (2001) *A Sunday at the Pool in Kigali,* A.Knopf: New York.

Craig, D. & Porter, D. (2002) 'Poverty Reduction Strategy Papers: a New Convergence', *World Development,*

30(12), http://www.adb.org/Poverty/PRS_Paper_30_Nov.pdf

Donors Group on Public Sector Reform (2002) *Improving Service Delivery Through Public Service Reform: Lessons of Experience from Select Sub-Saharan Africa Countries*, OECD DAC: Paris.

Drop the Debt (2001) *Reality Check: the Need for Deeper Debt Cancellation and the Fight Against HIV/AIDS*, www.jubileeusa.org

Ellis, F & James, R. (2002) *Keeping People Poor: Rural Poverty Reduction and Fiscal Decentralisation in Uganda and Tanzania*, www.chronicpoverty.org

EURODAD (2003) *User Guide to the PRGF Matrix*, www.eurodad.org

Global Campaign for Education (2003) 'World Bank to 'Actively Oppose' User Fees', www.campaignforeducation.org

Grindle, M (2003) *Good Enough Governance: Poverty Reduction and Reform in Developing Countries*, Harvard University.

International Monetary Fund (2003) *Joint Statement by the Government of Zambia and the IMF Staff Mission*, July 31, http://www.imf.org/external/np/sec/pr/2003/pr03132.htm

Jadhav, N. (2002) *Synopses of External Comments and Contributions to the Joint IMF/World Bank Staff Review of the PRSP Approach*, IMF/World Bank: Washington.

Kalima, B.(2003) *The HIPC Initiative: Experiences of Implementation in Africa*, AFRODAD, http://www.un.org/esa/coordination/ecosoc/Kalima.pdf

Madavo, C. (2001) 'HIPC and Beyond: Challenges for Africa', Address to European Union Parliament, Brussels, September 13.

Madavo, C. (2002) 'Sub-Saharan Africa', Development Cooperation Forum, Atlanta.

Malaluan, J. & Guttal, S. (2003), *Poverty Reduction Strategy Papers: a Poor Package for Poverty Reduction*, Focus on the Global South, www.focusweb.org

Pegg, S. (2003) *Poverty reduction or Poverty Exacerbation? World Bank Group support for extractive industries in Africa*, A report Sponsored by Oxfam America, Friends of the Earth – US, Environmental Defense, Catholic Relief Services and the Bank Information Center, http://www.bicusa.org/africa/Poverty_Reduction_Poverty_Exacerbation.pdf

Nampanya-Serpell, N. (2001) *Children Orphaned by HIV/AIDS in Zambia: Social and Economic Risk Factors of Premature Parental Death,* Nordic Africa Institute, Uppsala, Sweden.

PRMPR (Poverty Reduction Group) (2003) *A User's Guide to Poverty and Social Impact Analysis,* www.worldbank.org/psia

PRSP Monitoring and Synthesis Project (2003), ODI Project funded by DFID: www.prspsynthesis.org.

Publish What You Pay Campaign: www.publishwhatyoupay.org

Sarbib, J-L. (2000) in *The Namibian,* 15th May.

Sender, J. (2000) 'Reassessing the Role of the World Bank in Sub-Saharan Africa', in J. Pincus and J. Winter (eds) *Reinventing the World Bank*, Cornell University Press: Ithaca.

Stites, E, (2003) *Extractive Industries and Poverty Reduction Strategy Papers,* Commissioned by Oxfam America & Catholic Relief Services.

UNAIDS & UNDP (2000) *HIV/AIDS & Human Development South Africa.* http://www.undp.org.za/docs/pubs/hdr.overview.htm

UNCTAD (2002) *Economic Development in Africa: From Adjustment to Poverty Reduction: What is New?* UNCTAD: Geneva.

USAID (2003) *2004 Congressional Budget Justification for Zambia,* http://www.usaid.gov/policy/budget/cbj2004/sub-saharan_africa/Zambia.pdf

Chapter 9

African Conflicts, Colonialism and Contemporary Intervention

William Reno

Contemporary African states are products of European intervention and the importation of a now universal form of political organization from its European heartland. Nearly every state that currently exists in Africa reflects European conquest and imperial administration in boundaries and institutions. Often portrayed as chaotic, the entire continent is remarkable for having retained the international boundaries of the 1880s essentially unchanged. The challenge, especially since Independence has concerned how to refashion what Bertrand Badie (2000) calls the 'imported state' into an arrangement that can assure order, that citizens take as legitimate, and that can convince the international community of sufficient performance on a growing list of criteria: human rights, efficient governance, and since the attack on the World Trade Center in New York on 11 September 2001, the capacity to control its territory and regulate transactions and movement across borders.

The imported state, however, faces trouble in Africa. The present conflict in Côte d'Ivoire is estimated to have killed about 12,000 people since its start in September 2002. Sierra Leone emerges out of an eleven-year war that saw the near total collapse of its government and the establishment of a UN trusteeship. Liberia's warlord-turned-President faced UN sanctions for interfering in wars in neighbouring countries. He fought in a war that killed about 8 percent of the country's population, then ran Liberia as his personal fiefdom until international pressure forced him to flee to Nigeria in August. The UN monitors an uneasy peace in Guinea-Bissau since 1999. Guinea receives large numbers of refugees from neighbouring conflicts and faces political tensions of its own that governments and factions in the region exploit for their own ends. Nigeria regularly appears in international news media for its serious sectarian and ethnic violence. Congo and its neighbours remain embroiled in a conflict that destabilizes the entire region, despite a recent peace agreement. Zimbabwe's economy has shrunk to less than half its size in the mid 1990s. Somalia (or at least its southern half) still lacks a central government after more than a decade of on-going violence, and so on (Stockholm International Peace Research Institute 2003; United Nations 2002).

These countries experience the range of local and global forces that are responsible for state failure and conflict. Together they cast some doubt on the viability of the state system in this region. This chapter will assess outside efforts to reconstruct states, including armed intervention, democratization, economic reform, and the revival of new forms of trusteeship, and draw broader conclusions about the prospects for state reconstruction in Africa, especially in light of the recent trend of overseas intervention in Africa.

Global Causes of Failure

Some elements of conflict can be attributed to the ungluing of a colonial overlay on local societies. Colonial administrators and the new leaders who succeeded them found that to exercise power they had to co-opt local strongmen, grafting them into what initially appeared to be a fairly uniform system of state administration. What is remarkable is not the disorder in recent years; rather, it is that this colonial arrangement survived so long.

African and non-African leaders have good reasons to sustain what Robert Jackson calls 'quasi-states'. Quasi-states, he wrote, are "ex-colonial states that have been internationally enfranchised and possess the same rights and responsibilities as all other sovereign states" (Jackson 1990: 21). At the same time, they are unable, or lack the political will, to protect human rights, provide order, or promote the social or economic welfare of citizens. But in the interests of global order, the post-World War II idea of self-determination, and recognition in the 1950s and 1960s of the high costs of suppressing colonial rebellions, colonial states were turned into independent states, regardless.

'Self-determination of peoples' remains a cornerstone of the UN Charter. This is not self-determination for Mendes or Akan or Efik or Yoruba or Hausa or Kanuri. Rather, it means self-determination in the framework of colonial administration, handed over to local leaders. The victory of this version of self-determination is codified in the 1960 UN Declaration on the Granting of Independence to Colonial Countries and Peoples (Resolution 1514), which declared: "the inadequacy of political, economic, social or educational preparedness should never serve as a pretext for delaying independence".

This declaration faced its first test in 1960, as an army mutiny tore the Congo into several parts and government administration broke down days after independence. This also signalled the start of international attempts to resuscitate failed states, at that time in the form of a UN peacekeeping force.

Since then, states in Africa have become more difficult to maintain. Many scholars blame these problems on globalization. Global economic actors play a major role in violence in the region, but are not a *primary* cause of violence. Post-colonial states such as Singapore, United Arab Emirates, and South Korea have seized advantages in the world economy. But it appears that intensified global economic transactions help undermine already weak institutions in Africa. Rulers in these states discover that it is easier to manipulate cross-border transactions and regulations for the benefit of a political clique, often in coordination with global criminal enterprises, rather than for the interests of most citizens. IMF and World Bank-sponsored reforms that focus on dismantling state regulations and bureaucracies further undermine formal state capacities. In some instances, multi-party politics aggravates elite competition for spoils and is associated with further collapse and disorder.

This process might be 'normal', in that it might mark a syncretistic merging of European political forms with a reindigenization of political authority, much like the evolution of the Middle Kingdom into the modern sovereign state of China, or the Persian Empire's transformation into the state of Iran, or the bloody transition of predatory bandit organizations into political clans in Greece and a number of other countries.

Yet now more than in the past, states are essential building blocks of contemporary global society. There is no time for transition. The dangers that effectively stateless areas pose reinforce this assessment in Washington and elsewhere. This urgency brings with it a revival of Great Power tendency to divide the world, defining 'civilized states' as those that are capable of exercising a standard of control over their territories and sustain at least a minimal level of administration capable of carrying out tasks that Western states associate with governance. No longer are states accorded sovereignty by right. Such concerns appear in US President George W Bush's (2002) statement of a new security strategy:

> [t]he events of September 11, 2001 taught us that weak states, like Afghanistan, can pose as great a danger to our national interests as strong states. Poverty does not make poor people into terrorists and murderers. Yet poverty, weak institutions, and corruption can make weak states vulnerable to terrorist networks and drug cartels within their borders.

Stateless areas lack political structures amenable to the standard technologies of control - military, economic, bureaucratic - that others believe are necessary to avoid dangers. Lacking a state, how can one fight HIV/AIDS, suppress freelance armed militias or keep out terrorists? The costly military interventions of non-Africans in Somalia, Sierra Leone, Liberia, and Cote d'Ivoire show the depths of anxieties about this problem. Outcomes there also cast doubt on whether current remedies are capable of addressing this problem.

Internal Causes Of Failure

While the international environment plays a large role in shaping the process of state collapse, its causes are found in internal processes. These appear in 3 primary interactions, all of which are more common in Africa, compared to the rest of the world. These consist of a distinct political economy of what I call the 'Shadow State' (Reno 1995), alongside of the alienation of youth, and the politics of insurgency in Africa.

The political economy of state collapse often began as crisis management. Rulers who inherited weak institutional tools and who faced unruly local strongmen devised ingenious ways of reining in these forces, while meeting the post-colonial demands of citizens for more state services. But by the late 1960s, coups in Benin, Togo, Ghana, Nigeria, and Sierra Leone alerted incumbent leaders to the dangers they faced.

Armed coups showed rulers that strengthening state institutions to control unruly associates could empower rivals instead. Effective bureaucracies, a strong army - the customary path of adaptation to the European state system among reformers in Japan, Thailand, Iran and Turkey - thus posed much greater dangers to African leaders. This politics, not the economies or the specific distributions of resources made these places good candidates for state failure. Statistics from 1960 show no reason any of these places should suffer their present shortcomings. Ghana's living standards equalled South Korea's. Sierra Leone has the oldest Western style university in sub-Saharan Africa, Fourah Bay College, founded in 1827. Côte d'Ivoire boasted stable prosperity well into the 1980s.

Because of this institutional paradox, many rulers manage powerful political interests in ways that undermined their own state institutions. Taking advantage of the international norms that accorded them automatic recognition of sovereignty they turned states into façades behind which they accumulated wealth to build extensive patronage networks. Interventions into the economy, often as private businessmen, enabled politicians to use prerogatives of state power to accumulate more wealth. Control of the state enabled them to write laws and manipulate regulations to reward loyal political allies, a task usually at odds with providing for economic efficiency or widespread prosperity. Finally, control of the state equipped them to make deals with international businessmen, contract debts and receive foreign aid and military assistance.

Not surprisingly, this strategy of rule weakened other institutions of the state. As the demands of clients grew amidst ever present threats from rivals, real or imagined, there was less money to spend on health, education, or other services. The same logic of rule demanded the de-professionalization of militaries. Sierra Leone's Siaka Stevens, for example, only took office in 1968 after waiting a year for a counter-coup to throw out army officers who had seized power just as Stevens was to be sworn into office. The President barely survived a coup attempt in 1971. These, and other conspiracies, prompted the President to rely upon a collection of troops from neighbouring Guinea, armed youth gangs, and assorted military advisors from overseas. Among West Africa's 16 states, only Cape Verde and Senegal, have never had coups. The rest have had more than 30. This intentional abandonment of the state's monopoly of force - a characteristic of many countries in the region - fundamentally shaped conflicts that emerged in the 1990s as not only rebels, but multiple factions of its own military challenged governments.

Thus, when states such as Congo, Somalia, Liberia, Sierra Leone, Guinea-Bissau, and now Côte d'Ivoire have come under armed challenge, there is no real state in the sense of providing services to the public and exercising coercion to protect them. Instead, rebels emerge from among the plethora of private militaries connected to members of patronage networks. As the control of old patrons wanes, these entourages, as well as those who felt denied their rightful share of wealth, seized opportunities to rush to control these economic resources for themselves, ideally as the new claimant to the façade of state sovereignty. These armed groups therefore are not causes of state failure. Rather, they are products of states that had already collapsed, replaced with patronage politics rooted in the economy.

Prior to the start of fighting, collapsing state bureaucracies, and diminished capacity of governments left even committed officials unable to provide services to citizens. This puts most people, but especially youth, in an environment either of urban unemployment or what Paul Richards (1996) calls the 'rural slum', a shifting population of young people in a violent world, often drawn into armed networks of informal economies upon which politicians built their fortunes. Whether as diamond diggers in Sierra Leone, smugglers in Liberia or political muscle for Nigerian or Zimbabwean politicians, desperate youth end up as foot soldiers at the bottom of this fragmenting patronage politics. Deprived of economic opportunities outside the Shadow State sphere of political connections, these youth became recruits of would-be warlords.

The Sierra Leonean sociologist, Ibrahim Abdullah, also points to the emergence of alienated youthful intellectuals as key actors in conflict. As job opportunities disappeared or were possible only with Shadow State connections, educated youth rejected aspirations to join this corrupt elite, dreaming instead of radical alternatives, increasingly ones that have no place for states. They found their constituency among what he calls the 'lumpen proletarian' (Abdullah 1997) youth culture of the ruined economy. Scholars argue over the impact of urban and rural uneducated youth and alienated intellectuals on the course of conflicts, but their importance is widely recognized.

Finally, insurgents from neighbouring states feature in every conflict in Africa. Just in West Africa, UN investigators documented the role of the Liberian NPFL in training and arming Sierra Leone's RUF. The Government of Guinea supported Liberia's LURD, which recently fought its way to Liberia's capital. Likewise, Liberia's President

Taylor sponsored groups that destabilized Guinea. Cote d'Ivoire's war includes 2 rebel groups, Movement for Justice and Peace and the Popular Movement for the Greater West that signal in their names a connection to Liberia.

Finally, one should mention the very important role of France and its tacit alliance with agents of state decay in the region, especially Liberia's President Charles Taylor. French support bolstered him as a rebel leader in 1992, when the French Ambassador to Côte d'Ivoire paid him a visit. Taylor became a primary purveyor of instability now in Côte d'Ivoire and Guinea, and as noted earlier, was a key factor in prolonging Sierra Leone's war. This explains virulent anti-French sentiment in Côte d'Ivoire, where many people hold France responsible for the country's plight. This, coupled with France's protection of Rwanda's genocide regime in 1994, is a fascinating and horrible story. And as recently as January 2003, France's Government invited Charles Taylor to Paris in violation of UN sanctions against him and his government. Then in February 2003 Zimbabwe's Robert Mugabe received official French hospitality, despite EU sanctions against his regime.

Regardless of which factor is most responsible for West Africa's violence - Shadow State politics, youth alienation, or cross-border destabilization - all create conditions that are common to wars of state collapse. As such they shape the efforts of policy makers in Africa and outside the continent to formulate a response.

Outside Responses to State Failure and Conflict

In the context of the US experience with terrorism, but also within the recent evolution of international human rights and other legal norms, there is a growing non-African consensus that African states simply have to be rebuilt, given the high costs of state collapse. Large-scale migration, uncontrolled, often illicit, economic activity, and massive human rights violations become incubators for disorder, alongside the tendency for such consequences of state collapse to spread.

For hard-headed officials in distant ministries, concerns centre on the possibility that these places can become havens for terrorists, (one sees such justifications among Australian officials in explaining interventions in Papua New Guinea, East Timor and the Solomon Islands). That is, failure in one state threatens the security of other states, and if there are enough failed states in one region, they can weaken the orderly structure of states and the predictability and methods of control of populations that come with that state structure.

Those who support this perspective increasingly share interests with those who support more vigorous enforcement of international human rights and other legal norms. For them too, failure simply cannot be tolerated, and must be contained, if not reversed. The imposition of foreign courts, and even foreign administrations are justified if this will halt abuses.

The primary, and I believe unintended, consequence of this convergence is the imposition of a deeply conservative vision of world politics on Africa. As the 1815 Congress of Vienna declared that the turmoil of French-inspired radical republicanism must be contained behind a wall of perpetual autocratic monarchy, today's conflicts in Africa will be locked beneath the framework of the rejuvenated system of existing states.

Actions such as sanctions against 'conflict diamonds', arms embargos and so forth, address Africa's place in the global system of states and the world economy. Most remedies also involve open-ended commitments of overseas finance and personnel to build domestic African institutions. In this regard, conflict resolution efforts can be compared to massive interventions like the colonial project that created European style states in Africa in the first place. But is the current effort sustainable? The UN operation in Sierra Leone has cost about a billion dollars a year since 1999, this in a country with a GDP of US $650 million. French intervention in Cote d'Ivoire occupies 3,000 soldiers and consumes about a million Euros a day. Guinea-Bissau appears to rely upon UN and EU bureaucrats to run most essential state services, and to a lesser degree so do peaceful countries like Mali and Niger, where foreign aid has constituted the single largest source of government finance for the last decade.

Are alternative configurations possible? This is an interesting - and realistic - question but not one that the international community will soon entertain, especially if the US or Europe suffers a second spectacular terrorist attack. It is highly relevant, however, to ask this question, given the almost inevitable failure of the policies currently on the table.

Taken broadly, current global power politics and idealist efforts offer a 'Back to the Future' scenario as the international community (now multi-lateral instead of rival colonial powers) reoccupies African states, and builds them up (now with greater local participation) to be handed to African leaders. First, this includes the institution of 'democracy', defined as the restoration of order and institution of multiparty political competition with regular, usually internationally monitored elections. The second is 'good government', defined as the construction of institutions able to provide order and basic services to citizens. Third is 'economic liberalization', which demands that economies be organized along market principles with limited state intervention and management. This vision of what states should be in Africa is so deeply entrenched that there is virtually no consideration of alternatives. But is it successful? Let us look at each element of state restoration in turn.

Do international efforts result in the restoration of order stable enough to sustain formal democracy? This effort starts with re-professionalizing armies, precisely the opposite tack of Shadow State regimes. The record is not good in Sierra Leone or Liberia. Peace treaties in both countries featured provisions to re-build armies, only to see them fragment again and become instruments of ambitious contenders for power. A private company, Executive Outcomes (EO), did a fine job of training Sierra Leone's army in 1995-96, but this created tensions with parts of the military that were sidelined, as this always does. Training had no lasting positive impact. Eighty-nine days after EO left the country the army mutinied and joined with rebels to impose a 9-month reign of terror until a Nigerian expeditionary force kicked them out in 1998. After UN-sponsored training they rebelled exactly 1 day after the departure of the Nigerian force in 2000, only to be chased out again, this time by a British expeditionary force that remains in the country.

Are ethnic militias and home guards viable alternatives? Experience in most of Africa's wars and among Nigeria's ethnic militias show that they can protect supporters from attackers. But away from their kin they behave as bad or worse than rebels and fragmented armies. Remnants of national armies see them as competitors. Countries such as the former Yugoslavia, Somalia, Congo, and Sudan all have very unhappy human rights experiences with ethnic militias.

Democratic elections are a cornerstone of international mediation of conflicts. Most, however, follow disastrously damaging negotiations. Sierra Leone returned to war after the 1996 Abidjan Agreement and the 1999 Lome Agreement. Each agreement insisted on a place for rebels and army factions in peacetime governments at the insistence of outside mediators. Liberia's strongest warlord then used intimidation to get elected in 1997, and as I noted earlier, became a primary agent of regional destabilization.

Supporters of coalitions and comprehensive peace deals tout the experience of Mozambique in the early 1990s. There, however, RENAMO had no remaining external patron to whom it could turn to overturn the peace agreement. In fact, rebel-government negotiations usually fail, mostly because there is no viable power structure or institutions for participants to integrate into, a complaint rife among RENAMO's backers.

If outsiders are willing to force an agreement, then stay to guarantee its provisions, a 'peace settlement' can be imposed. Sierra Leone, for example, continues with its unusual, but widely accepted trusteeship under the direction of the former colonial power. Even so, January saw the flight of a militia leader from the capital to neighbouring Guinea, followed by what appeared to be staged riots in that country's capital. Sierra Leone's solution also relies on open-ended British willingness to maintain a protectorate in a part of the world in which it has no evident strategic or economic interests.

Economic revival is a distant glimmer. Sierra Leone and Liberia struggle along at about half to a third of their peak national incomes in the 1970s. Côte d'Ivoire's economy has lost a generation of progress, even if the country is peacefully unified now. It has proven difficult to revive effective state institutions capable of providing public services and promoting commerce. Sierra Leone's government collected only US $10 million in internal revenues in 2000, compared to about $250 million in the mid 1970s. About two-thirds of Liberia's US $60 million revenues in 2002 paid for the security details of President Taylor.

Effective reform requires dismantling the Shadow State, which means that local elites will have to give up their main sources of private wealth. This is likely to require very long-term direct outside control over the state, an effective recolonization. Agents of this trusteeship are likely to find themselves caught in battles between factions of this elite on whose behalf and for whose state they are supposedly acting.

CONCLUSION

These forces that undermine state restoration, especially the persistence of Shadow State economies and incumbent elites with substantial stakes in them, coupled with the tendency for insurgencies to operate across international borders, continue to counter-balance the rewards of state reconstruction, even given the substantial sums spent on this effort. There is no indication that the basic structures of state institutions will be restored in Africa's worst off states, at least not anytime soon. Order, democracy, and a growing economy are not going to occur under present conditions, no matter how much is spent or how ardent the wishful descriptions of imminent breakthroughs in World Bank reports.

This gloomy prognosis does not, however, characterize all of Africa. Nigeria managed to organize an election on 19 April 2003 that involved far less violence than many predicted. Nigeria's President may have many shortcomings, but a hidden success of his tenure has been the demobilization and disarming of substantial segments of the military. There are some glimmers that Nigeria's Federal Government is tackling the difficult problem of reorganizing police services. Throughout the country community associations mobilize to devise solutions to their own problems. Ijaw women learn that connecting with international environmental groups is a good way of pressing their demands for good governance where the exploitation of oil and fair distribution of its revenues is, as the great Nigerian scholar Claude Ake (1997) recognized, "the stuff of politics in Nigeria". For a time in late 2002, Christian and Muslim religious organizations in Kaduna were reining in armed groups of youths, and playing a big role in limiting the spread of sectarian violence.

Throughout Africa, people continue organizing or struggling to find solutions for the problems of state collapse. It is very typical though for many, especially those with access to outside resources, to promote restoration of states on their old foundations. In Africa's current position this is sensible; reorganization could open a Pandora's box of unanticipated (and nasty) outcomes. The reorganization of the Yugoslav political space was awful and unwelcome. In contrast, though it does not entirely suit comparison, the states that succeeded the Soviet Union offer promise to many.

Africa's overall re-configuration, on the other hand, will likely be more profound. Politics in many places is not based upon social structures that are conducive to building strong states. Maybe something else is required. The leaders of the United Arab Emirates succeeded in fooling the rest of the world into thinking they ruled a state, and it is accepted as such. But it is organized in very novel ways, and its leaders were able to exploit a particular period in world history that tolerated heterogeneity in political organization, a condition that no longer exists.

As for Africa, clearly not all of its states will collapse. But many of them have, and this process and the agents involved are not exceptional in this continent. Better then to ask the question of how to get from here to there, and study how people on the continent get it done, rather than to go back to an idealized version of what went before.

References

Abdullah, I. (1997) 'Bush Path to Destruction: The Origins and Character of the Revolutionary United Front (RUF/SL)', *Africa Development,* 22(3), pp. 45-76.

Ake, C. (1997) *Why Humanitarian Emergencies Occur: Insights from the Interface of State, Democracy, and Civil Society*, Helsinki: United Nations University.

Badie, B. (2000) *The Imported State: The Westernization of the Political Order*, Stanford, CA: Stanford University Press.

Bush, G. W. (2002) *The National Security Strategy of the United States of America,* Washington, DC: The White House, available at http://www.whitehouse.gov/nsc/nss.html

Jackson, R. (1990) *Quasi-States: Sovereignty, International Relations and the Third World,* New York: Cambridge University Press.

Reno, W. (1995) *Corruption and State Politics in Sierra Leone,* New York: Cambridge University Press.

Richards, P. (1996) *Fighting for the Forest: War, Youth, and Resources in Sierra Leone*, Portsmouth, NH: Heinemann Press.

Stockholm International Peace Research Institute, (2003), *Armaments, Disarmament and International Society,* New York: Oxford University Press;

United Nations, (2002) *Final Report of the Panel of Experts on the Illegal Exploitation of Natural Resources and Other Forms of Wealth in the Democratic Republic of Congo,* New York: UN, 8 October, paragraph 96.

Contributors

Colin Cameron is currently completing his doctoral thesis entitled "Negationism, Revisionism and the Rwandan Genocide" at The University of Queensland.

Jane Gilbert has extensive experience as a Clinical Psychologist within Mental Health Services in the UK and as a Consultant for the Centre for Mental Health Services Development (England). She has also lived and travelled in Africa for many years. Jane has been freelance since 2001 and was recently appointed Visiting Senior Lecturer, University College, Winneba, Ghana. She specialises in the design and delivery of workshops/training on psychological and mental health issues in cross cultural contexts, and has worked in the UK, The Gambia, Uganda, Lesotho and Ghana.

Jeremy Martens is a lecturer in History at the University of Western Australia. He has a PhD from Queens University and specialises in global history, South African, African and imperial history, and the history of race and racism. He has published various articles on South African history.

Edith Miguda is currently completing her doctoral studies on "International Catalysts and Women's Political Empowerment" at the University of Adelaide. She was formerly a lecturer in the Department of History and Government at the University of Nairobi, Kenya. She has published articles on African women, Women and Politics in Kenya and on Women, Peace and Conflict Resolution in Africa.

Eric Louw is Senior Lecturer in the School of Journalism & Communication, University of Queensland. He has PhD from the Centre for Cultural & Media Studies, University of Natal (Durban) and an MA in Political Science from the University of South Africa. He is the author of *The Media and Cultural Production*; *South African Media Policy*, and he co-authored *The South African Alternative Press*.

Tanya Lyons is a lecturer in African Studies and Globalisation at Flinders University in South Australia. She is the author of *Guns and Guerilla Girls: Women in the Zimbabwean Liberation Struggle*, and has published widely on the issues of globalisation, gender and Africa.

Geralyn Pye is a lecturer in the School of Political and International Studies at Flinders University where she teaches Development Studies and Latin American Studies. She is the author of *Sport in Cuba: The Diamond in the Rough*, and has published a number of chapters and articles on Development and Latin America.

William Reno is Associate Professor of Political Science at Northwestern University in the USA. He is the author of *Warlord Politics and African States* and writes widely on the topic of the political economy of state collapse, non-official local governance, and insurgency.

Teresa Thorp is a doctoral candidate at the Centre de Droit International, Européen et Comparé, Université Paris V, Sorbonne. Her research focuses on International Trade Law, notably Regional Implications of Trade, Global Competition Law & Institutional Reform, and Regime Change in Telecoms. She has a 20-year background in ICT development, of which 10 years has been spent at the executive level advising on ICT reform in global markets.

Helen Ware is Professor of International Agency Leadership at the University of New England in Armidale NSW. She was formerly Australian High Commissioner to Zambia, Malawi and Namibia and Ambassador to Angola. Prior to her return to academia, Helen Ware was an adviser to AusAID dealing with both bilateral and multilateral aid issues including negotiating with the World Bank.

Index